TABLE OF CONTENTS

2	INTRODUCTION
3	APPETIZERS AND DIPS
10	BREADS AND PASTRIES
24	MEAT AND POULTRY DISHES
37	RICE, PASTA, AND GRAIN DISHES
44	SEAFOOD DISHES
55	SOUPS AND LEGUMES
60	SWEETS AND DESSERTS
71	VEGETABLE AND SALAD DISHES
83	STORIES SECTION
88	HEALTH AND NUTRITION INFORMATION
89	COOKING TIPS AND TECHNIQUES
91	RECIPE INDEX

Dear Readers,

Welcome to a culinary exploration that transcends mere recipes and ingredients. This book invites you on a gastronomic journey to Ikaria, an enchanting island where food is an embodiment of culture, history, and a celebrated way of life.

Nestled in the Aegean Sea, Ikaria is not just known for its breathtaking landscapes and vibrant traditions, but also for its extraordinary cuisine. This cuisine is more than just sustenance; it's a tapestry of flavors, a testament to the island's rich history, and a key to its residents' famed longevity.

As you turn these pages, you will discover dishes that have been passed down through generations, each recipe telling a story of the island's past and present. From the simplicity of 'Fava' to the complexity of 'Gemista', each dish reflects the resourcefulness and creativity of the Ikarian people. Their use of fresh, locally sourced ingredients highlights a deep connection with the land and sea, a connection that is both nurturing and nourishing.

But this book is more than just a collection of recipes; it's an invitation to experience the Ikarian way of life. Through the stories accompanying each dish, you will get a glimpse of the communal spirit that defines mealtime in Ikaria. Here, cooking and eating are acts of joy and celebration, a means to connect with family, friends, and nature.

Moreover, the health benefits of these dishes are profound, aligning with the principles of the Mediterranean diet, renowned for its positive impact on longevity and well-being. As you explore these recipes, you'll also uncover the secrets to a healthier lifestyle, one that Ikarians have embraced for centuries.

Whether you are a seasoned chef or a culinary novice, these recipes are designed to inspire and delight. Each dish, from appetizers to desserts, is presented with easy-to-follow instructions, ensuring that the essence of Ikarian cuisine can be recreated in your kitchen.

So, let us embark on this delicious journey together. Embrace the flavors, the stories, and the spirit of Ikaria. Let every recipe take you closer to understanding the heart of this extraordinary island and its people.

APPETIZERS AND DIPS
The Essence of Ikarian Gatherings

Introduction to Ikarian Appetizers and Dips
The appetizers and dips of Ikaria are a delightful prelude to any meal, embodying the island's culinary philosophy of simplicity and flavor. Rooted in the traditions of the Mediterranean and the local bounty, these starters are not just food; they represent a way of life that prioritizes health, community, and enjoyment.

The Heart of Ikarian Cuisine
The recipes in this chapter, carefully selected to represent the heart of Ikarian cuisine, showcase the island's love for fresh, wholesome ingredients. Each recipe, from the creamy Taramosalata to the vibrant Beetroot and Yogurt Dip, is a testament to the island's culinary philosophy: food that nourishes both the body and the soul.

Simplicity and Nutrition Hand in Hand
Ikarian appetizers are a blend of simplicity and nutrition. The ingredients, be it the lush greens for the Zucchini Fritters or the fresh herbs in the various dips, are sourced locally, ensuring that they are as nutritious as they are flavorful. This adherence to local and fresh produce not only enhances the taste but also ensures that each dish is packed with natural goodness.

A Tribute to Traditional Cooking Techniques
The cooking techniques employed in Ikarian cuisine are steeped in tradition, focusing on enhancing the natural flavors rather than overpowering them. These methods passed down through generations, are evident in the straightforward yet skilled preparation of dishes like the Eggplant Dip and the Cheese and Yogurt Dip with Herbs.

Communal Eating: A Cultural Staple
In Ikaria, food is a communal affair. Appetizers and dips are often served family-style, encouraging sharing and conversation. This communal aspect of dining is central to the Ikarian way of life, where meals are as much about nourishing relationships as they are about nourishing the body.

Conclusion
Chapter 1 offers a glimpse into the heart of Ikarian cuisine, where each appetizer and dip is a celebration of local ingredients, traditional cooking, and communal eating. These recipes are not just a way to start a meal but are an integral part of the Ikarian culinary and cultural identity, inviting you to savor and share in the joy of simple, wholesome food.

RECIPES

- **Aginares a la Polita:** A heartwarming artichoke dish that brings the essence of spring to your table.
- **Chickpea Fritters:** Crispy on the outside, and tender on the inside, these fritters are a testament to the versatility of chickpeas.
- **Fava:** A creamy and smooth dip made from yellow split peas, garnished with onion and capers.
- **Kaparosalata:** A tangy and refreshing caper salad, perfect for a summer day.
- **Melitzanosalata:** A smoky eggplant dip that captures the essence of grilled eggplant.
- **Pantzaria:** A vibrant beetroot salad, rich in color and nutrients.
- **Riganada:** A simple yet flavorful dish of bread, tomato, and oregano.
- **Saganaki:** A deliciously fried cheese that is both crispy and gooey.
- **Skordalia:** A garlic-infused potato dip, perfect with bread or vegetables.
- **Skordostoumbi:** A spicy and aromatic dish, showcasing the robust flavors of garlic and tomato.
- **Tzatziki:** A refreshing yogurt and cucumber dip, a staple in Ikar cuisine.

SERVINGS: 4   PREPPING TIME: 20 MIN   COOKING TIME: 35 MIN

AGINARES A LA POLITA

INGREDIENTS

8 artichokes, cleaned and quartered
1 large onion, finely chopped
1 large carrot, sliced
1 potato, cubed
1/4 cup olive oil
Juice of 2 lemons
1/4 cup all-purpose flour
1 liter vegetable broth
1/2 cup chopped dill
Salt and pepper to taste

DIRECTIONS

1. In a large pot, heat the olive oil over medium heat and sauté the onion until translucent.
2. Add the artichokes, carrot, and potato to the pot. Cook for 5 minutes, stirring occasionally.
3. Sprinkle the flour over the vegetables and stir well to coat.
4. Gradually pour in the vegetable broth, stirring constantly to prevent lumps.
5. Bring to a boil, then reduce heat and simmer for about 25 minutes or until the vegetables are tender.
6. Remove from heat, add the lemon juice, dill, salt, and pepper. Stir well and let it stand for a few minutes before serving.

Nutritional Information (approximation per serving)*: Calories: 250, Protein: 6g, Carbohydrates: 35g, Fat: 12g, Fiber: 10g, Cholesterol: 0mg, Sodium: 500mg, Potassium: 800mg.

SERVINGS: 6   PREPPING TIME: 15 MIN (SOAKING TIME)   COOKING TIME: 10 MIN

CHICKPEA FRITTERS

INGREDIENTS

2 cups chickpeas, soaked overnight and drained
1 large onion, finely chopped
2 cloves garlic, minced
1/4 cup fresh parsley, chopped
1 teaspoon ground cumin
Salt and pepper to taste
Olive oil for frying

DIRECTIONS

1. In a food processor, combine the chickpeas, onion, garlic, parsley, and cumin. Process until mixture is smooth.
2. Season with salt and pepper, then form the mixture into small patties.
3. Heat olive oil in a frying pan over medium heat. Fry the patties for about 3-4 minutes on each side, or until golden brown and crispy.
4. Drain on paper towels and serve hot.

SERVINGS: 4   PREPPING TIME: 10 MIN   COOKING TIME: 60 MIN

FAVA

INGREDIENTS

2 cups yellow split peas, rinsed
1 large onion, finely chopped
2 cloves garlic, minced
1/4 cup olive oil
Juice of 1 lemon
4 cups water
Salt and pepper to taste
Chopped parsley and olive oil for serving

DIRECTIONS

1. In a large pot, combine the split peas, onion, garlic, and water.
2. Bring to a boil, then reduce heat and simmer for about 1 hour or until the split peas are very tender and the mixture has thickened.
3. Remove from heat and stir in the olive oil and lemon juice. Season with salt and pepper.
4. Use an immersion blender or food processor to puree the mixture until smooth.
5. Serve warm, garnished with chopped parsley and a drizzle of olive oil.

Nutritional Information (approximation per serving)*: Calories: 300, Protein: 10g, Carbohydrates: 45g, Fat: 10g, Fiber: 12g, Cholesterol: 0mg, Sodium: 400mg, Potassium: 600mg
Nutritional Information (approximation per serving)*: Calories: 350, Protein: 20g, Carbohydrates: 50g, Fat: 10g, Fiber: 15g, Cholesterol: 0mg, Sodium: 300mg, Potassium: 900mg

SERVINGS: 4   PREPPING TIME: 15 MIN   COOKING TIME: 0 MIN

KAPAROSALATA

INGREDIENTS

1 cup capers, rinsed and drained
2 medium tomatoes, finely chopped
1 small red onion, finely chopped
1/4 cup kalamata olives, pitted and chopped
2 tablespoons fresh parsley, chopped
1/4 cup extra virgin olive oil
2 tablespoons red wine vinegar
Salt and pepper to taste

DIRECTIONS

1. In a large mixing bowl, combine capers, tomatoes, red onion, olives, and parsley.
2. In a small bowl, whisk together olive oil and red wine vinegar. Pour over the caper mixture.
3. Gently toss to combine. Season with salt and pepper to taste.
4. Let it sit for about 10 minutes to allow flavors to meld before serving.

SERVINGS: 4   PREPPING TIME: 10 MIN   COOKING TIME: 45 MIN

MELITZANOSALATA

INGREDIENTS

2 large eggplants
2 cloves garlic, minced
1/4 cup extra virgin olive oil
2 tablespoons fresh lemon juice
2 tablespoons fresh parsley, chopped
Salt and pepper to taste

DIRECTIONS

1. Preheat your oven to 400°F (200°C). Prick eggplants with a fork and place on a baking sheet.
2. Bake for 35-45 minutes or until tender. Remove from oven and let cool.
3. Peel the skin off the eggplants and place the flesh in a colander to drain excess liquid.
4. In a bowl, mash the eggplant with a fork. Stir in garlic, olive oil, and lemon juice.
5. Season with salt and pepper. Garnish with chopped parsley before serving.

Nutritional Information (approximation per serving)*: Calories: 180, Protein: 2g, Carbohydrates: 10g, Fat: 15g, Fiber: 3g, Cholesterol: 0mg, Sodium: 420mg, Potassium: 250mg.
Nutritional Information (approximation per serving)*: Calories: 220, Protein: 3g, Carbohydrates: 18g, Fat: 16g, Fiber: 9g, Cholesterol: 0mg, Sodium: 10mg, Potassium: 690mg.

SERVINGS: 4   PREPPING TIME: 10 MIN   COOKING TIME: 45 MIN

PANTZARIA

INGREDIENTS

4 medium beets, cooked and sliced
2 cloves garlic, minced
1/4 cup red wine vinegar
1/4 cup extra virgin olive oil
1/2 teaspoon sugar
Salt and pepper to taste
2 tablespoons fresh parsley, chopped
2 tablespoons walnuts, chopped (optional)

DIRECTIONS

1. If using fresh beets, boil them in water for about 45 minutes or until tender. Let them cool, peel, and slice.
2. In a large bowl, mix sliced beets, garlic, red wine vinegar, olive oil, and sugar.
3. Toss until the beets are well coated. Season with salt and pepper.
4. Chill in the refrigerator for at least 1 hour.
5. Before serving, sprinkle with fresh parsley and optional chopped walnuts.

SERVINGS: 4   PREPPING TIME: 10 MIN   COOKING TIME: 5 MIN

RIGANADA

INGREDIENTS

14 slices of crusty bread
2 ripe tomatoes, finely chopped
1/4 cup extra virgin olive oil
1 garlic clove, halved
2 teaspoons dried oregano
Salt and pepper to taste
Feta cheese, crumbled (optional)
Kalamata olives, pitted and halved (optional)

DIRECTIONS

1. Toast the bread slices until they are golden brown.
2. Rub each slice of toast with the cut side of the garlic clove.
3. Top each slice with chopped tomatoes, drizzle with olive oil, and sprinkle with oregano, salt, and pepper.
4. If desired, add crumbled feta cheese and a few Kalamata olives on top.
5. Serve immediately while the toast is still warm and crisp.

Nutritional Information (approximation per serving)*: Calories: 200, Protein: 3g, Carbohydrates: 14g, Fat: 14g, Fiber: 4g, Cholesterol: 0mg, Sodium: 180mg, Potassium: 400mg.
Nutritional Information (approximation per serving)*: Calories: 250, Protein: 5g, Carbohydrates: 24g, Fat: 15g, Fiber: 3g, Cholesterol: 0mg, Sodium: 360mg, Potassium: 200mg.

SERVINGS: 4   PREPPING TIME: 5 MIN   COOKING TIME: 5 MIN

SAGANAKI

INGREDIENTS

8 oz firm cheese (e.g., kefalotyri or halloumi), cut into thick slices
1/2 cup all-purpose flour
1/4 cup olive oil
Lemon wedges for serving

DIRECTIONS

1. Dredge the cheese slices in flour, shaking off any excess.
2. Heat the olive oil in a frying pan over medium heat.
3. Fry the cheese for about 2 minutes on each side or until golden brown and crispy.
4. Remove from the pan and drain on paper towels.
5. Serve hot with lemon wedges on the side.

SERVINGS: 4   PREPPING TIME: 15 MIN   COOKING TIME: 0 MIN

SKORDOSTOUMBI

INGREDIENTS

4 slices of stale bread, crusts removed and soaked in water
6 cloves garlic, minced
1/2 cup extra virgin olive oil
2 tablespoons red wine vinegar
Salt and pepper to taste

DIRECTIONS

1. Squeeze the water out of the soaked bread and place it in a bowl.
2. Add the minced garlic to the bread and mash together until well combined.
3. Gradually add the olive oil, continuously stirring until the mixture becomes smooth and thick.
4. Stir in the red wine vinegar, and season with salt and pepper to taste.
5. Serve as a spread or dip with fresh vegetables or crusty bread.

Nutritional Information (approximation per serving)*: Calories: 400, Protein: 20g, Carbohydrates: 10g, Fat: 32g, Fiber: 0g, Cholesterol: 90mg, Sodium: 820mg, Potassium: 60mg.
Nutritional Information (approximation per serving)*: Calories: 300, Protein: 3g, Carbohydrates: 18g, Fat: 24g, Fiber: 2g, Cholesterol: 0mg, Sodium: 200mg, Potassium: 50mg.

SERVINGS: 4   PREPPING TIME: 15 MIN   COOKING TIME: 20 MIN
(IF USING POTATOES)

SKORDALIA

INGREDIENTS

1 cup mashed potatoes or 1 cup of soaked and drained almonds or walnuts
4 cloves garlic, minced
1/2 cup extra virgin olive oil
2 tablespoons white wine vinegar
Salt to taste

DIRECTIONS

1. If using potatoes, boil them until tender, drain, and mash until smooth.
2. In a mortar and pestle or food processor, combine garlic and a pinch of salt, mashing until you have a paste.
3. Combine the garlic paste with the mashed potatoes or ground nuts in a mixing bowl.
4. Gradually add olive oil and vinegar, mixing continuously. The texture should be creamy and smooth.
5. Season with salt to taste and serve with bread or as a condiment.

SERVINGS: 4   PREPPING TIME: 15 MIN   COOKING TIME: 0 MIN

TZATZIKI

INGREDIENTS

2 cups Greek yogurt
1 cucumber, grated and drained
2 cloves garlic, minced
2 tablespoons extra virgin olive oil
1 tablespoon white wine vinegar
1 tablespoon fresh dill, chopped
Salt and pepper to taste

DIRECTIONS

1. Combine the Greek yogurt, grated cucumber, minced garlic, olive oil, and white wine vinegar in a bowl.
2. Mix thoroughly until all ingredients are well combined.
3. Stir in the chopped dill, and season with salt and pepper to taste.
4. Chill in the refrigerator for at least 1 hour to allow flavors to meld.
5. Serve cold with pita bread, fresh vegetables, or as a condiment for grilled meats.

Nutritional Information (approximation per serving)*: Calories: 300, Protein: 2g, Carbohydrates: 15g, Fat: 25g, Fiber: 2g, Cholesterol: 0mg, Sodium: 10mg, Potassium: 350mg.
Nutritional Information (approximation per serving)*: Calories: 150, Protein: 9g, Carbohydrates: 8g, Fat: 9g, Fiber: 1g, Cholesterol: 5mg, Sodium: 150mg, Potassium: 250mg.

BREADS AND PASTRIES
The Artisanal Heartbeat of Ikarian Cuisine

In the quaint kitchens of Ikaria, breads and pastries are more than just food; they are a celebration of life and tradition. Each loaf of bread and every pastry embodies the essence of Ikarian culinary art, deeply rooted in the rich heritage of the island.

The Rustic Charm of Ikarian Bread
The tradition of bread-making in Ikaria is an age-old practice, passed down through generations. The simplicity of the ingredients - flour, water, yeast, and salt - belies the skill and patience required to create the perfect loaf. The rustic, crusty loaves are a common sight, often baked in wood-fired ovens that infuse them with a unique, smoky flavor.

Pastries: A Symphony of Flavors
Ikarian pastries are a symphony of flavors and textures. From the flaky layers of the classic Spinach and Feta Pie to the sweet, syrupy goodness of Honey-Soaked Pastries, these delicacies are a testament to the versatility and creativity of Ikarian baking. Each recipe tells a story, whether it's a family gathering, a religious celebration, or a simple daily pleasure.

Local Ingredients: The Essence of Authenticity
The secret to the distinctive taste of Ikarian breads and pastries lies in the locally sourced ingredients. The island's olive oil, renowned for its quality, lends a rich, earthy flavor to the dough, while the locally grown herbs add a fragrant, fresh dimension to both savory and sweet creations.

Nurturing Community Through Baking
In Ikaria, baking is a communal affair, a time for sharing stories and skills. The kneading of dough and the aroma of freshly baked bread have a way of bringing people together, symbolizing unity and the shared joys of life.

Health and Nutrition: The Ikarian Way
Aligned with Ikaria's reputation for health and longevity, these breads and pastries are not just delightful to the palate but also nourishing for the body. Made with whole grains, fresh produce, and minimal processing, they embody the principles of a diet that promotes longevity and well-being.

Cooking Tips and Techniques:
Bread and pastry doughs benefit from patient and thorough kneading to develop texture and flavor.

Utilizing local ingredients like fresh herbs, cheeses, and olive oil enhances the authenticity and taste of each recipe.

Health and Nutrition Information:
The breads and pastries: incorporate elements of the Mediterranean diet known for its health benefits. Whole grains, olive oil, and fresh produce used in these recipes contribute to a balanced and nutritious diet.

Final Thoughts
This chapter not only offers a collection of cherished recipes but also invites readers to immerse themselves in the wholesome and communal spirit of Ikarian life. Each recipe is a narrative in itself, a piece of the island's soul, shared through the universal language of delicious, heartwarming food.

RECIPES

- **Boureki:** A savory pastry filled with a delightful blend of cheese and vegetables, representing the island's love for fresh, local produce.
- **Choriatiko Psomi:** The quintessential village bread, hearty and full of flavor, embodying the simplicity of Ikarian cuisine.
- **Eliopsomo:** An olive bread that combines the richness of local olives with the traditional bread-making techniques of the island.
- **Flaounes:** Traditional cheese-filled pastries that are a staple during Ikarian Easter, symbolizing festivity and community.
- **Kleftiko Pita:** A "stolen" pie filled with mouth-watering meat and herbs, reminiscent of the island's history and tales of survival.
- **Kreatopita:** A savory meat pie that showcases the island's love for hearty and satisfying meals.
- **Kotopita Icaria:** A unique Ikarian spin on the classic chicken pie, using local herbs and spices.
- **Kremmydopita:** An onion pie that perfectly balances sweetness and savoriness, a testament to the island's resourcefulness.
- **Ladenia:** Ikaria's version of pizza, topped with tomatoes, onions, and olive oil, reflecting the island's simplicity and love for sharing.
- **Myzithropitakia:** Small cheese pies filled with myzithra cheese, offering a glimpse into the island's dairy traditions.
- **Pitarakia:** Small pies filled with greens and herbs, showcasing the island's abundant natural produce.
- **Prasopita:** A leek pie that perfectly combines the sweetness of leeks with savory fillings.
- **Psomi me Elies:** A bread enriched with olives, encapsulating the essence of the Mediterranean diet.
- **Sfouggato:** A traditional omelette pie, blending eggs with local vegetables for a nutritious meal.
- **Tsoureki:** A sweet, braided bread, often enjoyed during celebrations, symbolizing joy and togetherness.

SERVINGS: 6 PREPPING TIME: 20 MIN COOKING TIME: 60 MIN

BOUREKI

INGREDIENTS
3 medium zucchinis, thinly sliced
3 large potatoes, thinly sliced
1 large onion, thinly sliced
2 cups crumbled feta cheese
1/2 cup fresh mint, chopped
1/2 cup olive oil
Salt and pepper to taste
Phyllo dough sheets

DIRECTIONS
1. Preheat oven to 180°C (350°F). Grease a baking dish.
2. Layer half of the potato slices in the bottom of the dish. Season with salt and pepper.
3. Layer half of the zucchini slices over the potatoes. Add a layer of onion slices.
4. Sprinkle half of the feta cheese and mint over the onions.
5. Repeat the layers with the remaining potatoes, zucchini, onions, feta, and mint.
6. Drizzle with olive oil. Cover the top with phyllo dough sheets, tucking the edges inside the dish. Brush the top with olive oil. Bake for 60 minutes, or until golden and the vegetables are tender. Let it cool slightly before serving.

SERVINGS: 6 PREPPING TIME: 20 MIN (PLUS 1-2 HOURS FOR RISING) COOKING TIME: 30-35 MIN

ELIOPSOMO

INGREDIENTS
4 cups all-purpose flour
1 tablespoon dry yeast
1 teaspoon sugar
1 1/2 cups warm water
2 teaspoons salt
1/4 cup extra virgin olive oil
1 cup Kalamata olives, pitted and chopped
2 tablespoons fresh rosemary, chopped
Extra flour for dusting

DIRECTIONS
1. Dissolve yeast and sugar in 1/2 cup warm water. Set aside for 10 minutes until frothy.
2. In a large bowl, mix flour and salt. Add yeast mixture, olive oil, remaining water, olives, and rosemary.
3. Knead on a floured surface for 10 minutes until smooth. Place in an oiled bowl, cover, and let rise for 1-2 hours.
4. Preheat oven to 400°F (200°C). Punch down dough, shape into a loaf, place on a baking tray, and let rest for 30 minutes. Bake for 30-35 minutes. Cool on a wire rack.

Nutritional Information (approximation per serving)*: Calories: 350, Protein: 10g, Carbohydrates: 30g, Fat: 22g, Fiber: 4g, Cholesterol: 30mg, Sodium: 400mg, Potassium: 700mg.
Nutritional Information (approximation per serving)*: Calories: 350, Protein: 10g, Carbohydrates: 58g, Fat: 10g, Fiber: 4g, Cholesterol: 0mg, Sodium: 800mg, Potassium: 150mg.

SERVINGS: 6 — PREPPING TIME: 20 MIN (PLUS 1-2 HOURS FOR RISING) — COOKING TIME: 20-30 MIN

CHORIATIKO PSOMI

INGREDIENTS

4 cups all-purpose flour
1 tablespoon dry yeast
1 teaspoon sugar
1 1/2 cups warm water
2 teaspoons salt
2 tablespoons olive oil
Extra flour for dusting
A handful of mixed seeds (sesame, sunflower, poppy)
    for topping (optional)

DIRECTIONS

1. In a small bowl, dissolve the yeast and sugar in 1/2 cup of the warm water. Set aside for 10 minutes, until it becomes frothy.
2. In a large mixing bowl, combine the flour and salt. Make a well in the center and add the yeast mixture, olive oil, and gradually add the remaining water.
3. Mix to form a soft dough. Knead the dough on a floured surface for about 10 minutes, until it is smooth and elastic.
4. Place the dough in an oiled bowl, cover with a damp cloth, and leave it to rise in a warm place for 1-2 hours, or until it doubles in size.
5. Preheat your oven to 400°F (200°C).
6. Punch down the dough, shape it into a round loaf, and place it on a baking tray lined with parchment paper. Sprinkle with mixed seeds if using.
7. Bake for 30-40 minutes, or until the bread sounds hollow when tapped on the bottom.
8. Let it cool on a wire rack before slicing.

Nutritional Information (approximation per serving)*: Calories 320, Protein 9 g, Carbohydrates 60 g, Fat 4 g, Fiber 3 g, Cholesterol 0 mg, Sodium 780 mg, Potassium 100 mg.

SERVINGS: 16 PASTRIES **PREPPING TIME: 30 MIN (PLUS 2-3 HOURS FOR RISING)** **COOKING TIME: 30 MIN**

FLAOUNES

INGREDIENTS

4 cups all-purpose flour
1 packet (7g) active dry yeast
1/4 cup sugar
1/4 cup warm milk
1/2 cup unsalted butter, melted
2 large eggs, beaten
1/2 cup halloumi cheese, grated
1/2 cup feta cheese, crumbled
1/2 cup cheddar cheese, grated
1/4 cup fresh mint, chopped
1/4 cup fresh parsley, chopped
1/4 cup sesame seeds for topping (optional)

DIRECTIONS

1. In a small bowl, dissolve the yeast and sugar in warm milk. Set aside for 10 minutes until frothy.
2. In a large mixing bowl, combine the flour, melted butter, and beaten eggs.
3. Add the yeast mixture to the flour mixture and mix until a dough forms.
4. Knead the dough for about 5 minutes until smooth. Cover and let it rise in a warm place for 2-3 hours or until it doubles in size.
5. Preheat your oven to 350°F (175°C).
6. In a separate bowl, mix together the grated halloumi, crumbled feta, cheddar cheese, chopped mint, and parsley.
7. Punch down the dough and divide it into 16 equal portions.
8. Flatten each portion into a small circle and place a spoonful of the cheese mixture in the center.
9. Fold the dough over the filling and seal the edges to form a triangle or square pastry.
10. Place the pastries on a baking tray lined with parchment paper. Optionally, sprinkle with sesame seeds.
11. Bake for 25-30 minutes or until the pastries are golden brown.
12. Let them cool before serving.

Nutritional Information (approximation per serving)*: Calories: 240, Protein: 7g, Carbohydrates: 27g, Fat: 12g, Fiber: 1g, Cholesterol: 55mg, Sodium: 240mg, Potassium: 100mg.

SERVINGS: 4	PREPPING TIME: 20 MIN	COOKING TIME: 45 MIN

KLEFTIKO PITA

INGREDIENTS

1 pound ground lamb
1 small onion, finely chopped
2 cloves garlic, minced
1/4 cup fresh parsley, chopped
1 teaspoon dried oregano
Salt and pepper to taste
6 sheets phyllo pastry
1/4 cup melted butter
1/4 cup breadcrumbs

DIRECTIONS

1. Preheat your oven to 350°F (175°C).
2. In a skillet, cook the ground lamb over medium heat until browned. Remove excess fat.
3. Add the chopped onion and minced garlic to the skillet. Cook until the onion is translucent.
4. Stir in the fresh parsley, dried oregano, salt, and pepper. Remove from heat.
5. Place one sheet of phyllo pastry on a clean surface and brush it with melted butter. Sprinkle with breadcrumbs.
6. Repeat this process, stacking three sheets on top of each other with butter and breadcrumbs between each layer.
7. Spread the lamb mixture evenly over the top sheet.
8. Fold in the sides of the phyllo pastry and roll it up to form a log.
9. Place the log in a baking dish and brush the top with more melted butter.
10. Bake for 45 minutes or until the pastry is golden brown and crispy.
11. Slice and serve hot.

Nutritional Information (approximation per serving)*: Calories: 450, Protein: 20g, Carbohydrates: 20g, Fat: 30g, Fiber: 1g, Cholesterol: 85mg, Sodium: 350mg, Potassium: 280mg.

SERVINGS: 6   PREPPING TIME: 30 MIN   COOKING TIME: 45 MIN

KREATOPITA

INGREDIENTS

1 pound ground beef or lamb
1 onion, finely chopped
2 cloves garlic, minced
1/2 cup fresh parsley, chopped
1/4 cup fresh mint, chopped
1/4 cup breadcrumbs
1/4 cup extra virgin olive oil
Salt and pepper to taste
1 package phyllo pastry sheets
Butter for brushing

DIRECTIONS

1. Preheat your oven to 350°F (175°C). In a large skillet, heat the olive oil over medium heat. Add the chopped onion and garlic and sauté until translucent.
2. Add the ground meat and cook until browned. Drain excess fat if needed.
3. Stir in the fresh parsley, fresh mint, breadcrumbs, salt, and pepper. Remove from heat.
4. Layer 4-5 sheets of phyllo pastry in a greased baking dish, brushing each layer with melted butter. Spread the meat mixture evenly over the phyllo layers.
5. Cover with another 4-5 sheets of phyllo, brushing each layer with butter.
6. Score the top of the pie with a sharp knife into serving portions.
7. Bake for 40-45 minutes or until the pie is golden brown and crispy.
8. Let it cool slightly before slicing and serving.

Nutritional Information (approximation per serving)*: Calories: 420, Protein: 20g, Carbohydrates: 20g, Fat: 30g, Fiber: 2g, Cholesterol: 60mg, Sodium: 480mg, Potassium: 200mg.

SERVINGS: 4   PREPPING TIME: 30 MIN   COOKING TIME: 45 MIN

KOTOPITA ICARIA

INGREDIENTS

2 tablespoons olive oil
1 onion, finely chopped
2 cloves garlic, minced
1 pound boneless, skinless chicken breasts, cut into small pieces
1/2 cup carrots, diced
1/2 cup green peas
1/2 cup bell peppers, diced (red and green)
1/2 cup tomatoes, diced
1 teaspoon dried oregano
Salt and pepper to taste
1 package phyllo pastry sheets
1/4 cup melted butter
1/4 cup breadcrumbs

DIRECTIONS

1. Preheat your oven to 350°F (175°C).
2. In a large skillet, heat the olive oil over medium heat. Add the chopped onion and sauté until translucent.
3. Add the minced garlic and sauté for another minute until fragrant.
4. Add the chicken pieces and cook until they start to brown.
5. Stir in the diced carrots, green peas, bell peppers, tomatoes, dried oregano, salt, and pepper. Cook until the vegetables are tender and the chicken is cooked through.
6. Remove the skillet from heat and let the mixture cool.
7. Lay out one sheet of phyllo pastry and brush it with melted butter. Sprinkle with breadcrumbs.
8. Repeat this process, stacking three sheets on top of each other with butter and breadcrumbs between each layer.
9. Spoon the chicken and vegetable mixture onto the pastry sheets.
10. Fold in the sides of the phyllo pastry and roll it up to form a log.
11. Place the log in a baking dish and brush the top with more melted butter.
12. Bake for 45 minutes or until the pastry is golden brown and crispy.
13. Slice and serve hot.

Nutritional Information (approximation per serving)*: Calories: 400, Protein: 25g, Carbohydrates: 25g, Fat: 23g, Fiber: 3g, Cholesterol: 75mg, Sodium: 450mg, Potassium: 480mg.

SERVINGS: 6   PREPPING TIME: 30 MIN   COOKING TIME: 40 MIN

KREMMYDOPITA

INGREDIENTS

4 large onions, thinly sliced
1/4 cup extra virgin olive oil
1/2 cup feta cheese, crumbled
1/2 cup Greek yogurt
3 large eggs, beaten
2 tablespoons fresh dill, chopped
Salt and pepper to taste
8 sheets phyllo pastry
Butter for brushing

DIRECTIONS

1. Preheat your oven to 350°F (175°C).
2. In a large skillet, heat the olive oil over medium heat. Add the thinly sliced onions and sauté until caramelized and golden brown.
3. In a mixing bowl, combine the crumbled feta cheese, Greek yogurt, beaten eggs, fresh dill, salt, and pepper.
4. Add the caramelized onions to the mixture and stir well.
5. Grease a baking dish and layer 4 sheets of phyllo pastry, brushing each sheet with melted butter.
6. Spread the onion and cheese mixture evenly over the phyllo layers.
7. Cover with another 4 sheets of phyllo, brushing each sheet with butter.
8. Score the top of the pie into serving portions with a sharp knife.
9. Bake for 35-40 minutes or until the pie is golden brown and set.
10. Let it cool slightly before slicing and serving.

Nutritional Information (approximation per serving)*: Calories: 320, Protein: 10g, Carbohydrates: 26g, Fat: 21g, Fiber: 2g, Cholesterol: 135mg, Sodium: 380mg, Potassium: 210mg.

SERVINGS: 6   PREPPING TIME: 20 MIN   COOKING TIME: 30 MIN

LADENIA

INGREDIENTS
2 cups all-purpose flour
1 packet (7g) dry yeast
1 teaspoon sugar
1/2 cup warm water
1/4 cup extra virgin olive oil
2 large tomatoes, thinly sliced
1 red onion, thinly sliced
1 tablespoon dried oregano
Salt and pepper to taste

DIRECTIONS
1. In a small bowl, dissolve the yeast and sugar in warm water. Set aside for 10 minutes until frothy. In a large mixing bowl, combine the flour and a pinch of salt. Make a well in the center and add the yeast mixture and olive oil. Mix to form a soft dough.
2. Knead the dough for about 5 minutes until smooth, then cover and let it rest for 10 min.
3. Preheat your oven to 375°F (190°C). 5. Divide the dough into 6 equal portions and roll each portion into a flat oval shape.
4. Place the dough ovals on baking trays lined with parchment paper.
5. Arrange the tomato and onion slices on top of each oval, drizzle with olive oil, and sprinkle with dried oregano, salt, and pepper. Bake for 20-25 minutes or until the dough is golden and the toppings are tender. Serve warm.

SERVINGS: 4   PREPPING TIME: 20 MIN   COOKING TIME: 20 MIN

MYZITHROPITAKIA

INGREDIENTS
1 cup myzithra cheese (or ricotta cheese)
1/4 cup feta cheese, crumbled
1 egg
1 tablespoon fresh mint, chopped
1 package phyllo pastry sheets
1/4 cup unsalted butter, melted

DIRECTIONS
1. Preheat your oven to 350°F (175°C). In a mixing bowl, combine the myzithra cheese, feta cheese, egg, and fresh mint. Mix until well blended.
2. Cut the phyllo pastry sheets into squares (approximately 4x4 inches).
3. Place a small spoonful of the cheese mixture in the center of each pastry square.
4. Fold the squares into triangles, sealing the edges with melted butter.
5. Place the triangles on a baking tray lined with parchment paper, and brush the tops with more melted butter. Bake for 15-20 minutes or until the pastries are golden and crisp. Serve warm or at room temperature.

Nutritional Information (approximation per serving)*: Calories: 250, Protein: 5g, Carbohydrates: 35g, Fat: 10g, Fiber: 3g, Cholesterol: 0mg, Sodium: 220mg, Potassium: 150mg.
Nutritional Information (approximation per serving)*: Calories: 280, Protein: 10g, Carbohydrates: 15g, Fat: 20g, Fiber: 1g, Cholesterol: 95mg, Sodium: 480mg, Potassium: 60mg.

SERVINGS: 4   PREPPING TIME: 30 MIN   COOKING TIME: 25 MIN

PITARAKIA

INGREDIENTS

1 cup cooked rice
1/2 cup feta cheese, crumbled
1/4 cup fresh dill, chopped
1/4 cup fresh parsley, chopped
1 egg
1 package phyllo pastry sheets
1/4 cup unsalted butter, melted

DIRECTIONS

1. Preheat your oven to 350°F (175°C).
2. In a mixing bowl, combine the cooked rice, crumbled feta cheese, fresh dill, fresh parsley, and egg. Mix until well combined.
3. Cut the phyllo pastry sheets into squares (approximately 4x4 inches).
4. Place a spoonful of the rice mixture in the center of each pastry square.
5. Fold the squares into triangles, sealing the edges with melted butter.
6. Place the triangles on a baking tray lined with parchment paper, and brush the tops with more melted butter. Bake for 20-25 minutes or until the pastries are golden and crispy. Serve warm or at room temperature.

SERVINGS: 4   PREPPING TIME: 20 MIN   COOKING TIME: 20 MIN

PRASOPITA

INGREDIENTS

2 leeks, thinly sliced
1/4 cup extra virgin olive oil
1 cup feta cheese, crumbled
1/4 cup fresh dill, chopped
1/4 cup fresh parsley, chopped
4 eggs
Salt and pepper to taste
1 package phyllo pastry sheets
Butter for brushing

DIRECTIONS

1. Preheat your oven to 350°F (175°C). In a large skillet, heat the olive oil over medium heat. Add the thinly sliced leeks and sauté until tender and slightly caramelized.
2. In a mixing bowl, combine the sautéed leeks, crumbled feta cheese, fresh dill, fresh parsley, eggs, salt, and pepper. Mix well.
3. Cut the phyllo pastry sheets into squares (approximately 4x4 inches).
4. Place a spoonful of the leek mixture in the center of each pastry square.
5. Fold the squares into triangles, sealing the edges with melted butter.
6. Place the triangles on a baking tray lined with parchment paper, and brush the tops with more melted butter. Bake for 35-40 minutes or until the pies are golden brown and set.

Nutritional Information (approximation per serving)*: Calories: 320, Protein: 8g, Carbohydrates: 30g, Fat: 20g, Fiber: 1g, Cholesterol: 120mg, Sodium: 420mg, Potassium: 90mg.
Nutritional Information (approximation per serving)*: Calories: 280, Protein: 9g, Carbohydrates: 18g, Fat: 19g, Fiber: 2g, Cholesterol: 170mg, Sodium: 360mg, Potassium: 170mg.

SERVINGS: 1 LOAF | PREPPING TIME: 20 MIN / RISE TIME: 1 HOUR 30 MIN | COOKING TIME: 30-35 MIN

PSOMI ME ELIES

INGREDIENTS

3 cups all-purpose flour
1 1/2 teaspoons salt
1 1/4 cups warm water (about 110°F or 43°C)
1 packet (7g) active dry yeast
1 teaspoon sugar
1 cup Kalamata olives, pitted and chopped
1/4 cup extra virgin olive oil
1 tablespoon fresh rosemary, chopped (optional)
Additional olives for garnish (optional)

DIRECTIONS

1. In a small bowl, combine the warm water, sugar, and yeast. Let it sit for about 5-10 minutes until frothy. In a large mixing bowl, whisk together the flour and salt.
2. Pour the yeast mixture into the flour mixture and stir to form a shaggy dough.
3. Add the chopped Kalamata olives to the dough and knead them in until they are evenly distributed. Knead the dough on a floured surface for about 5-7 minutes until it becomes smooth and elastic.
4. Place the dough in a lightly oiled bowl, cover with a clean kitchen towel, and let it rise in a warm place for 1 hour or until it has doubled in size.
7. Preheat your oven to 375°F (190°C).
8. Punch down the risen dough to remove excess air.
9. Shape the dough into a round or oval loaf and place it on a baking sheet lined with parchment paper.
10. If desired, brush the top of the loaf with extra virgin olive oil and sprinkle with fresh rosemary. You can also press additional olives into the surface for garnish.
11. Bake for 30-35 minutes or until the bread is golden brown and sounds hollow when tapped on the bottom.
12. Allow the bread to cool before slicing and serving.

Nutritional Information (approximation per serving)*: Calories: 220, Protein: 3g, Carbohydrates: 23g, Fat: 13g, Fiber: 2g, Cholesterol: 0mg, Sodium: 440mg, Potassium: 80mg.

SERVINGS: 4　　PREPPING TIME: 10 MIN　　COOKING TIME: 30 MIN

SFOUGGATO

INGREDIENTS

4 large zucchinis, thinly sliced
1 onion, finely chopped
4 eggs
1/4 cup feta cheese, crumbled
2 tablespoons fresh dill, chopped
2 tablespoons fresh parsley, chopped
Salt and pepper to taste
2 tablespoons extra virgin olive oil

DIRECTIONS

1. Preheat your oven to 350°F (175°C).
2. In a large skillet, heat the olive oil over medium heat. Add the chopped onion and sauté until translucent.
3. Add the thinly sliced zucchinis and continue to cook until they are tender and slightly caramelized. Remove from heat.
4. In a mixing bowl, beat the eggs and add the crumbled feta cheese, fresh dill, fresh parsley, salt, and pepper. Mix well.
5. Add the sautéed zucchinis and onion to the egg mixture and stir to combine.
6. Grease a baking dish and pour the mixture into it.
7. Bake for 25-30 minutes or until the top is golden brown and the center is set.
8. Serve warm or at room temperature.

Nutritional Information (approximation per serving)*: Calories: 220, Protein: 9g, Carbohydrates: 11g, Fat: 16g, Fiber: 3g, Cholesterol: 190mg, Sodium: 390mg, Potassium: 440mg.

SERVINGS: 2 LOAVES   PREPPING TIME: 30 MIN   COOKING TIME: 30 MIN
RISE TIME: 2 HOURS

TSOUREKI

INGREDIENTS

4 1/2 cups all-purpose flour
1/2 cup warm milk (about 110°F or 43°C)
2 packets (14g) active dry yeast
1 cup sugar
4 large eggs
1/2 cup unsalted butter, softened
1 teaspoon vanilla extract
1/2 teaspoon ground mahlab (optional, for flavor)
1/4 teaspoon ground mastiha (optional, for flavor)
1/4 teaspoon salt
1 egg yolk (for egg wash)
Sliced almonds or sesame seeds for decoration (optional)

DIRECTIONS

1. In a small bowl, combine the warm milk and one packet of active dry yeast. Add a pinch of sugar, stir, and let it sit for about 10 minutes until frothy.
2. In a large mixing bowl, whisk together the flour and the remaining sugar.
3. In a separate bowl, beat the eggs and add them to the flour mixture along with the softened butter, vanilla extract, ground mahlab (if using), ground mastiha (if using), and salt.
4. Pour the yeast mixture into the bowl and mix to form a sticky dough.
5. Knead the dough on a floured surface for about 10-15 minutes until it becomes smooth and elastic.
6. Place the dough in a lightly oiled bowl, cover with a clean kitchen towel, and let it rise in a warm place for 1-2 hours or until it has doubled in size.
7. Preheat your oven to 350°F (175°C).
8. Divide the dough into two equal portions and shape each into a long rope.
9. Twist the ropes together to form a braided loaf.
10. Place the Tsoureki on a baking sheet lined with parchment paper.
11. Beat the egg yolk and brush it over the top of the Tsoureki. Decorate with sliced almonds or sesame seeds if desired.
12. Bake for 25-30 minutes or until the bread is golden brown and sounds hollow when tapped on the bottom.
13. Allow the Tsoureki to cool before slicing and serving.

Nutritional Information (approximation per serving)*: Calories: 240 (per slice), Protein: 6g, Fat: 7g, Fiber: 1g, Carbohydrates: 38g, Cholesterol: 50mg, Sodium: 50mg, Potassium: 75mg

MEAT AND POULTRY DISHES
The Savory Delights of Ikarian Cuisine

In the heart of the Mediterranean, Ikaria's cuisine offers a tantalizing array of meat and poultry dishes that reflect a blend of tradition and rich, savory flavors. This chapter delves into the heartwarming world of these dishes, each carrying the essence of Ikaria's culinary heritage.

A Reflection of the Island's Landscape
The meat and poultry recipes of Ikaria mirror the island's diverse landscape, with ingredients and cooking methods that have evolved to make the best use of local produce. From the mountainous terrains to the lush valleys, the natural environment plays a pivotal role in shaping these dishes.

Celebrating Local Produce and Simple Techniques
Ikaria's approach to meat and poultry is about celebrating the local produce and employing simple, time-honored cooking techniques. Whether it's a slow-cooked stew or a grilled delicacy, the emphasis is always on enhancing the natural flavors, rather than overpowering them.

Stews and Braises: A Symphony of Flavors
Stews and braises are staples in Ikarian cuisine, known for their depth of flavor. Ingredients like tomatoes, onions, garlic, and a variety of herbs are used generously to create rich, satisfying dishes that are as nutritious as they are delicious.

Grilled Delights: Savoring the Simplicity
Grilling is another popular method, especially for poultry. The simplicity of grilling allows the quality of the meat to shine through, complemented by the subtle use of herbs and spices that are characteristic of Ikarian cooking.

Health and Nutrition: A Balanced Approach
Consistent with the island's philosophy of healthy living, meat, and poultry dishes in Ikaria are often balanced with abundant fresh vegetables, legumes, and whole grains, ensuring a nutritious and well-rounded meal.

A Testament to Ikarian Hospitality
These recipes are not just about sustenance; they are a testament to Ikarian hospitality and the island's culture of sharing. Meals are often enjoyed communally, bringing families and friends together in a celebration of life's simple pleasures.

Cooking Tips and Techniques
Slow cooking is key to developing deep flavors in dishes like Kleftiko and Stifado.
Fresh herbs and spices are essential in enhancing the flavors of meat and poultry dishes.
Emphasize lean cuts of meat and poultry for healthier options.
Traditional slow-cooking methods are key to tender and flavorful stews and casseroles.
Grilling is a preferred method for dishes like Souvlaki and Gyros, enhancing the meat's natural flavors.

Health and Nutrition Information
This chapter balances the indulgence of meat dishes with a focus on health, aligning with Ikaria's reputation as a Blue Zone. Recipes are adapted to be lower in fat and calories without sacrificing flavor, showcasing how meat and poultry can be part of a balanced and nutritious diet. These dishes are often accompanied by fresh vegetables and salads, aligning with the principles of the Blue Zone and the Mediterranean diet for a wholesome and nutritious meal.

The use of fresh herbs and spices not only adds depth to each dish but also boosts its nutritional profile.

In Conclusion This chapter is more than just a compilation of recipes; it's an invitation to explore the rich tapestry of flavors and traditions that make Ikarian meat and poultry dishes so special. Each recipe is a window into the soul of the island, offering a taste of its vibrant culture and timeless culinary traditions.

RECIPES

- **Giaourtlou:** A dish that perfectly marries meat with yogurt, showcasing the harmonious blend of robust and delicate flavors.
- **Gyros:** A lighter version of the classic Greek gyro, made with lean meats and served with fresh, wholesome ingredients.
- **Lachanodolmades:** Cabbage rolls stuffed with a flavorful meat mixture, symbolizing the island's resourcefulness and love for comfort food.
- **Keftedes:** Savory meatballs that are a staple in Ikarian cuisine, reflecting the simplicity and richness of the island's gastronomy.
- **Kleftiko:** A lamb dish rich with herbs, reflecting the pastoral traditions and tales of the island.
- **Kotopoulo me Hilopites:** Chicken with traditional Ikarian pasta, a dish that brings warmth and comfort to any Ikarian table.
- **Kotopoulo me Rizi:** A classic chicken and rice dish that's a beloved family favorite, offering both simplicity and hearty satisfaction.
- **Kouneli Stifado:** A rabbit stew with a rich, aromatic sauce, epitomizing the island's love for game and hearty stews.
- **Moussaka:** A layered eggplant and meat casserole topped with creamy béchamel, a quintessential representation of Ikarain culinary art.
- **Ntolmadakia me Kima:** Grape leaves stuffed with seasoned meat, a dish that's as much a part of Ikarian culture as it is a culinary delight.
- **Patatato:** A meat and potato stew that's a staple in Ikarian festivities, known for its heartiness and depth of flavor.
- **Patsas:** A traditional tripe soup believed to have restorative properties, reflecting the island's appreciation for nose-to-tail eating.
- **Piperia Gemisti:** Stuffed bell peppers, a colorful and flavorful dish that celebrates the island's bountiful produce.
- **Psaronefri me Damaskina:** Pork tenderloin with prunes, a dish that beautifully balances sweet and savory elements.
- **Soutzoukakia:** Spiced meatballs in a rich tomato sauce, a dish with historical roots and a taste that tells a story of cultural fusion.
- **Souvlaki:** Skewered and grilled meat, marinated in herbs and spices, offering a healthier take on this popular street food.
- **Stifado:** A traditional Ikarian stew with meat and shallots, known for its rich flavor and tender texture.
- **Tigania:** A quick-fried pork dish, often enjoyed as a meze, showcasing the island's love for simple yet flavorful preparations.
- **Yemista me Kima:** Stuffed vegetables with a meat filling, a dish that's a celebration of the island's agricultural heritage and culinary creativity.

SERVINGS: 4   PREPPING TIME: 20 MIN   COOKING TIME: 40 MIN

GIAOURTLOU

INGREDIENTS

500 g lamb, cut into small cubes
2 tablespoons olive oil
1 onion, finely chopped
2 garlic cloves, minced
1 teaspoon paprika
1/2 teaspoon cumin
Salt and pepper to taste
4 pita breads
2 cups Greek yogurt
1 tablespoon butter
Fresh parsley, chopped for garnish

DIRECTIONS

1. Heat olive oil in a pan over medium heat. Add lamb cubes and cook until browned.
2. Add onion and garlic, cooking until softened. Season with paprika, cumin, salt, and pepper. Reduce heat and cook until lamb is tender, about 30 minutes.
3. Warm pita breads in the oven or on a grill. Spread Greek yogurt on each pita bread, then top with lamb mixture. In a small saucepan, melt butter and drizzle over the lamb.
4. Garnish with chopped parsley before serving.

SERVINGS: 6   PREPPING TIME: 30 MIN   COOKING TIME: 45 MIN

LACHANODOLMADES

INGREDIENTS

1 large head of cabbage
1 cup brown rice, cooked
1/2 lb (about 225g) ground lean meat (beef, pork, or turkey)
1 large onion, finely chopped
2 cloves garlic, minced
1/4 cup fresh dill, chopped
1/4 cup fresh parsley, chopped
1 egg, beaten
2 tablespoons olive oil
1 lemon, juice and zest
Salt and pepper to taste
2 cups vegetable broth

DIRECTIONS

1. Carefully remove leaves from the cabbage head, blanch them in boiling water for a few minutes, then drain. In a bowl, combine cooked rice, ground meat, onion, garlic, dill, parsley, egg, lemon zest, salt, and pepper.
2. Place a spoonful of the filling on each cabbage leaf, fold sides in, and roll up.
3. In a large pot, arrange the cabbage rolls in layers. Drizzle with olive oil and lemon juice.
4. Pour vegetable broth over the rolls, bring to a boil, then reduce heat and simmer for about 45 minutes. Serve hot, with additional lemon wedges if desired.

Nutritional Information (approximation per serving)*: Calories: 600, Protein: 35g, Carbohydrates: 45g, Fat: 30g, Fiber: 2g, Cholesterol: 100mg, Sodium: 600mg, Potassium: 500mg.
Nutritional Information (approximation per serving)*: Calories: 250, Protein: 15g, Carbohydrates: 25g, Fat: 10g, Fiber: 5g, Cholesterol: 50mg, Sodium: 300mg, Potassium: 500mg.

SERVINGS: 4   PREPPING TIME: 20 MIN   COOKING TIME: 15 MIN

GYROS

INGREDIENTS

- 1 pound boneless skinless chicken breasts or lean pork loin, thinly sliced
- 4 whole wheat pita bread or flatbreads
- 1 cup Greek yogurt (for tzatziki sauce)
- 1 cucumber, grated (for tzatziki sauce)
- 2 cloves garlic, minced (for tzatziki sauce)
- Juice of 1 lemon (for tzatziki sauce)
- 1 tablespoon fresh dill, chopped (for tzatziki sauce)
- 1 red onion, thinly sliced
- 1 tomato, thinly sliced
- 1/2 cup fresh parsley leaves
- Olive oil for cooking
- Salt and pepper to taste

DIRECTIONS

1. In a bowl, mix together the Greek yogurt, grated cucumber, minced garlic, lemon juice, and chopped dill to prepare the tzatziki sauce. Refrigerate the sauce until ready to use.
2. Season the thinly sliced chicken or pork with salt, pepper, and a drizzle of olive oil.
3. Preheat a grill or grill pan over medium-high heat.
4. Grill the chicken or pork slices for about 3-4 minutes on each side, or until cooked through and slightly charred.
5. Warm the whole wheat pita bread or flatbreads on the grill for a minute on each side.
6. Assemble the gyros by placing a portion of the grilled meat on each warm pita bread. Top with sliced red onion, tomato, and fresh parsley.
7. Drizzle the tzatziki sauce over the gyros.
8. Fold the pita bread around the filling and serve immediately.

Nutritional Information (approximation per serving)*: Calories: 350 per serving, Protein: 30g, Fat: 12g, Fiber: 4g, Carbohydrates: 30g, Cholesterol: 70mg, Sodium: 350mg, Potassium: 450mg.

SERVINGS: 4   PREPPING TIME: 20 MIN   COOKING TIME: 20 MIN

KEFTEDES

INGREDIENTS

1 pound ground beef or lamb
1 small onion, finely chopped
2 cloves garlic, minced
1/4 cup fresh parsley, chopped
1/4 cup fresh mint, chopped
1/2 cup breadcrumbs
1 egg
1 teaspoon dried oregano
Salt and pepper to taste
Vegetable oil for frying

DIRECTIONS

1. In a mixing bowl, combine the ground meat, chopped onion, minced garlic, fresh parsley, fresh mint, breadcrumbs, egg, dried oregano, salt, and pepper.
2. Mix the ingredients together until well combined. Shape the mixture into small meatballs, about the size of golf balls. Heat vegetable oil in a skillet over medium-high heat.
3. Fry the meatballs in batches until they are browned on all sides and cooked through, about 10 minutes per batch. Drain the meatballs on paper towels to remove excess oil.
4. Serve hot with your choice of sauce or alongside pita bread and tzatziki.

SERVINGS: 4   PREPPING TIME: 20 MIN   COOKING TIME: 2 HOURS

KLEFTIKO

INGREDIENTS

1 pound lamb shoulder, cut into chunks
2 cloves garlic, minced
1 onion, chopped
1 red bell pepper, chopped
1 green bell pepper, chopped
2 tomatoes, diced
1/4 cup extra virgin olive oil
1 teaspoon dried oregano
1 teaspoon dried thyme
Salt and pepper to taste
1/4 cup white wine
Parchment paper or aluminum foil

DIRECTIONS

1. Preheat your oven to 350°F (175°C). In a large bowl, combine the lamb chunks, minced garlic, chopped onion, chopped red bell pepper, chopped green bell pepper, diced tomatoes, olive oil, dried oregano, dried thyme, salt, and pepper. Mix well.
2. Tear off four pieces of parchment paper or aluminum foil, large enough to wrap each portion. Divide the lamb mixture evenly among the parchment paper or foil pieces.
3. Fold and seal each parchment paper or foil packet, creating a tight seal.
4. Place the sealed packets on a baking sheet and bake in the preheated oven for 2 hours.
5. Carefully open the packets, drizzle white wine over the lamb, and serve hot.

Nutritional Information (approximation per serving)*: Calories: 300, Protein: 22g, Carbohydrates: 10g, Fat: 20g, Fiber: 1g, Cholesterol: 120mg, Sodium: 350mg, Potassium: 310mg.
Nutritional Information (approximation per serving)*: Calories: 400, Protein: 20g, Carbohydrates: 10g, Fat: 30g, Fiber: 2g, Cholesterol: 60mg, Sodium: 300mg, Potassium: 520mg.

SERVINGS: 4   PREPPING TIME: 15 MIN   COOKING TIME:

KOTOPOULO ME HILOPITES

INGREDIENTS

- 4 boneless, skinless chicken breasts
- 2 tablespoons olive oil
- 1 onion, chopped
- 2 cloves garlic, minced
- 1 cup Hilopites pasta (or egg noodles) ~~120g~~ 250g
- 1 cup chicken broth 250 ml
- 1 cup tomatoes, diced
- 1 teaspoon dried oregano
- Salt and pepper to taste
- Fresh parsley for garnish (optional)

DIRECTIONS

1. In a large skillet, heat the olive oil over medium heat. Add the chopped onion and sauté until translucent.
2. Add the minced garlic and sauté for another minute until fragrant.
3. Add the chicken breasts and cook until they are browned on both sides. Stir in the Hilopites pasta, chicken broth, diced tomatoes, dried oregano, salt, and pepper.
4. Cover the skillet and simmer for 20-25 minutes, or until the chicken is cooked through, and the pasta is tender. Garnish with fresh parsley if desired before serving.

SERVINGS: 4   PREPPING TIME: 15 MIN   COOKING TIME: 30 MIN

KOTOPOULO ME RIZI

INGREDIENTS

- 4 bone-in, skin-on chicken thighs
- 2 tablespoons olive oil
- 1 onion, chopped
- 2 cloves garlic, minced
- 1 cup long-grain rice
- 2 cups chicken broth
- 1 cup tomatoes, diced
- 1 teaspoon dried oregano
- Salt and pepper to taste
- Fresh lemon wedges for serving (optional)

DIRECTIONS

1. In a large skillet, heat the olive oil over medium-high heat. Add the chopped onion and sauté until translucent.
2. Add the minced garlic and sauté for another minute until fragrant.
3. Add the chicken thighs, skin side down, and cook until they are browned and crispy.
4. Stir in the long-grain rice, chicken broth, diced tomatoes, dried oregano, salt, and pepper.
5. Cover the skillet and simmer for 20-25 minutes, or until the chicken is cooked through, and the rice is tender. Serve with fresh lemon wedges if desired.

Nutritional Information (approximation per serving)*: Calories: 350, Protein: 30g, Carbohydrates: 30g, Fat: 12g, Fiber: 3g, Cholesterol: 75mg, Sodium: 400mg, Potassium: 550mg

Nutritional Information (approximation per serving)*: Calories: 400, Protein: 25g, Carbohydrates: 40g, Fat: 15g, Fiber: 2g, Cholesterol: 95mg, Sodium: 550mg, Potassium: 450mg.

SERVINGS: 4   PREPPING TIME: 20 MIN   COOKING TIME: 1 HOUR 30 MIN

KOUNELI STIFADO

INGREDIENTS

1 rabbit, cut into pieces
2 onions, chopped
2 cloves garlic, minced
2 tablespoons olive oil
1 cup red wine
1 can (14 ounces) diced tomatoes
1 cinnamon stick
3-4 cloves
1 bay leaf
1 teaspoon dried oregano
Salt and pepper to taste
Fresh parsley for garnish (optional)

DIRECTIONS

1. In a large pot or Dutch oven, heat the olive oil over medium heat. Add the chopped onions and sauté until translucent. Add the minced garlic and sauté for another minute until fragrant. Add the rabbit pieces and brown them on all sides.
2. Pour in the red wine and let it simmer for a few minutes to reduce.
3. Stir in the diced tomatoes, cinnamon sticks, cloves, bay leaf, dried oregano, salt, and pepper. Cover the pot and simmer over low heat for 1 hour, or until the rabbit is tender and the stew thickens. Garnish with fresh parsley if desired before serving.

SERVINGS: 4   PREPPING TIME: 20 MIN   COOKING TIME: 2 HOURS

NTOLMADAKIA ME KIMA

INGREDIENTS

30 grape leaves (or pickled grape leaves), drained and rinsed
500g ground beef or lamb
1 cup rice, uncooked
1 large onion, finely chopped
2 cloves garlic, minced
1/4 cup fresh parsley, chopped
1/4 cup fresh mint, chopped
1/2 cup olive oil
1 lemon, juice only
Salt and pepper to taste
2 cups water or broth

DIRECTIONS

1. In a bowl, mix together the ground meat, rice, onion, garlic, parsley, mint, half of the olive oil, lemon juice, salt, and pepper.
2. Place a grape leaf on a flat surface, shiny side down. Put a spoonful of the filling near the stem end. Fold the sides over the filling and roll up tightly into a cigar shape.
3. Arrange the rolls seam-side down in a large pot. Drizzle with remaining olive oil and add water or broth. Cover and simmer over low heat for about 60 minutes, until the filling is cooked and the rice is tender. Serve warm.

Nutritional Information (approximation per serving)*: Calories: 350, Protein: 30g, Carbohydrates: 10g, Fat: 10g, Fiber: 2g, Cholesterol: 90mg, Sodium: 400mg, Potassium: 450mg.
Nutritional Information (approximation per serving)*: Calories: 350, Protein: 20g, Carbohydrates: 30g, Fat: 18g, Fiber: 2g.

SERVINGS: 6   PREPPING TIME: 30 MIN   COOKING TIME: 1 HOUR

MOUSSAKA

INGREDIENTS

2 large eggplants, sliced
1 pound ground beef or lamb
1 onion, chopped
2 cloves garlic, minced
1 can (14 ounces) diced tomatoes
1 teaspoon dried oregano
Salt and pepper to taste
4 tablespoons olive oil
4 tablespoons butter
1/4 cup all-purpose flour
2 cups milk
1/4 teaspoon ground nutmeg
1/2 cup grated Parmesan cheese
2 eggs, beaten

DIRECTIONS

1. Preheat your oven to 375°F (190°C).
2. Place the sliced eggplants on a baking sheet, brush with olive oil, and bake for 20 minutes or until they become tender.
3. In a large skillet, heat the olive oil over medium heat. Add the chopped onion and sauté until translucent.
4. Add the minced garlic and sauté for another minute until fragrant.
5. Add the ground beef or lamb and cook until browned. Drain excess fat.
6. Stir in the diced tomatoes, dried oregano, salt, and pepper. Simmer for 15 minutes.
7. In a saucepan, melt the butter over medium heat. Stir in the flour and cook for 2 minutes to make a roux.
8. Gradually whisk in the milk to make a white sauce. Add the ground nutmeg and continue to cook until the sauce thickens.
9. In a separate bowl, beat the eggs and stir in half of the grated Parmesan cheese.
10. In a baking dish, layer the baked eggplant slices, followed by the meat sauce, and then the white sauce.
11. Repeat the layers and finish with the white sauce on top. Sprinkle the remaining Parmesan cheese.
12. Bake for 40-45 minutes or until the Moussaka is golden brown and bubbling.
13. Allow it to cool slightly before serving.

Nutritional Information (approximation per serving)*: Calories: 450, Protein: 20g, Carbohydrates: 20g, Fat: 30g, Fiber: 5g, Cholesterol: 120mg, Sodium: 500mg, Potassium: 680mg.

SERVINGS: 4 PREPPING TIME: 20 MIN COOKING TIME: 2 HOURS

PATATATO

INGREDIENTS

1 pound goat meat (or beef or lamb), cubed
4 potatoes, peeled and cut into chunks
1 onion, chopped
2 cloves garlic, minced
1/4 cup olive oil
1/2 cup red wine
1 cup canned diced tomatoes
1 teaspoon dried oregano
Salt and pepper to taste
Fresh parsley for garnish (optional)

DIRECTIONS

1. In a large pot, heat the olive oil over medium heat. Add the chopped onion and sauté until translucent. Add the minced garlic and sauté for another minute until fragrant.
2. Add the cubed goat meat (or beef or lamb) and brown it on all sides.
3. Pour in the red wine and let it simmer for a few minutes to reduce. Stir in the canned diced tomatoes, dried oregano, salt, and pepper. Add enough water to cover the meat and bring it to a boil.
4. Reduce the heat, cover the pot, and simmer for 1.5 to 2 hours, or until the meat becomes tender. Add the peeled and chunked potatoes to the pot and continue to simmer until they are cooked and the stew thickens. Adjust the seasoning with salt and pepper as needed. Garnish with fresh parsley if desired before serving.

SERVINGS: 6 PREPPING TIME: 30 MIN COOKING TIME: 1 HOUR

YEMISTA ME KIMA

INGREDIENTS

6 large tomatoes
6 bell peppers
500g ground beef or lamb
1 cup rice, uncooked
1 large onion, finely chopped
1/4 cup olive oil
2 cloves garlic, minced
1/2 cup fresh parsley, chopped
Salt and pepper to taste
1 cup water or broth

DIRECTIONS

1. Preheat the oven to 180°C (350°F). Cut the tops off the tomatoes and peppers and scoop out the insides.
2. In a bowl, mix the ground meat, rice, onion, garlic, parsley, half of the olive oil, salt, and pepper. Stuff the mixture into the tomatoes and peppers, and replace their tops.
3. Place them in a baking dish, drizzle with the remaining olive oil, and add water or broth to the dish. Bake for about 1 hour, until the vegetables are tender and the filling is cooked.

Nutritional Information (approximation per serving)*: Calories: 350, Protein: 25g, Carbohydrates: 30g, Fat: 14g, Fiber: 5g, Cholesterol: 80mg, Sodium: 450mg, Potassium: 900mg.
Nutritional Information (approximation per serving)*: Calories: 350, Protein: 25g, Carbohydrates: 30g, Fat: 14g, Fiber: 5g, Cholesterol: 80mg, Sodium: 450mg, Potassium: 900mg.

SERVINGS: 4   PREPPING TIME: 20 MIN   COOKING TIME: 3 HOURS

PATSAS

INGREDIENTS

1 pound tripe (cleaned and sliced)
2 onions, chopped
2 cloves garlic, minced
1/4 cup olive oil
1/4 cup red wine vinegar
1 teaspoon dried oregano
Salt and pepper to taste
Lemon wedges for serving (optional)

DIRECTIONS

1. In a large pot, heat the olive oil over medium heat. Add the chopped onions and sauté until translucent. Add the minced garlic and sauté for another minute until fragrant.
2. Add the sliced tripe and cook for a few minutes until it starts to brown.
3. Pour in the red wine vinegar and let it simmer for a few minutes.
4. Add enough water to cover the tripe, along with dried oregano, salt, and pepper.
5. Cover the pot and simmer over low heat for 3 hours, or until the tripe is tender.
6. Serve with lemon wedges if desired.

SERVINGS: 4   PREPPING TIME: 20 MIN   COOKING TIME: 1 HOUR

PIPERIA GEMISTI

INGREDIENTS

4 bell peppers, tops removed and seeded
1 cup rice, uncooked
500g ground beef or lamb
1 onion, finely chopped
2 cloves garlic, minced
1/4 cup fresh parsley, chopped
1/4 cup olive oil
1 can diced tomatoes
Salt and pepper to taste
1 cup water or broth

DIRECTIONS

1. Preheat the oven to 180°C (350°F).
2. In a bowl, mix the ground meat, rice, onion, garlic, parsley, half of the olive oil, salt, and pepper.
3. Stuff each bell pepper with the mixture and place in a baking dish.
4. Mix the diced tomatoes with the remaining olive oil and pour over and around the peppers. Add water or broth to the dish.
5. Cover with foil and bake for about 1 hour, until the peppers are tender and the filling is cooked through. Serve warm.

Nutritional Information (approximation per serving)*: Calories: 250, Protein: 20g, Carbohydrates: 10g, Fat: 12g, Fiber: 2g, Cholesterol: 100mg, Sodium: 350mg, Potassium: 350mg.
Nutritional Information (approximation per serving)*: Calories: 400, Protein: 22g, Carbohydrates: 45g, Fat: 18g, Fiber: 6g.

SERVINGS: 4   PREPPING TIME: 20 MIN   COOKING TIME: 45 MIN

PSARONEFRI ME DAMASKINA

INGREDIENTS

1 pound pork loin, cut into chunks
1 onion, chopped
2 cloves garlic, minced
1/2 cup dried plums (damaskina)
1/4 cup red wine
1 teaspoon dried thyme
Salt and pepper to taste
2 tablespoons olive oil
Fresh parsley for garnish (optional)

DIRECTIONS

1. In a skillet, heat the olive oil over medium-high heat. Add the chopped onion and sauté until translucent. Add the minced garlic and sauté for another minute until fragrant.
2. Add the pork chunks and cook until they are browned on all sides.
3. Stir in the dried plums (damaskina), dried thyme, salt, and pepper.
4. Pour in the red wine and let it simmer for a few minutes.
5. Reduce the heat, cover the skillet, and simmer for 30-45 minutes, or until the pork is cooked through and tender. Garnish with fresh parsley if desired before serving.

SERVINGS: 4   PREPPING TIME: 20 MIN   COOKING TIME: 1 HOUR 30 MIN

STIFADO

INGREDIENTS

1 pound beef stew meat, cubed
2 onions, chopped
2 cloves garlic, minced
1/4 cup olive oil
1 can diced tomatoes
1/4 cup red wine vinegar
1 teaspoon ground cinnamon
4-5 cloves
Salt and pepper to taste
Fresh parsley for garnish (optional)

DIRECTIONS

1. In a large pot, heat the olive oil over medium heat. Add the chopped onions and sauté until translucent. Add the minced garlic and sauté for another minute until fragrant.
2. Add the beef stew meat and brown it on all sides.
3. Pour in the red wine vinegar and let it simmer for a few minutes.
4. Stir in the diced tomatoes, ground cinnamon, cloves, salt, and pepper.
5. Add enough water to cover the meat and bring it to a boil.
6. Reduce the heat, cover the pot, and simmer for 1 to 1.5 hours, or until the beef becomes tender. Adjust the seasoning with salt and pepper as needed.
7. Garnish with fresh parsley if desired before serving.

Nutritional Information (approximation per serving)*: Calories: 350, Protein: 25g, Carbohydrates: 20g, Fat: 15g, Fiber: 3g, Cholesterol: 70mg, Sodium: 400mg, Potassium: 500mg.
Nutritional Information (approximation per serving)*: Calories: 400, Protein: 25g, Carbohydrates: 15g, Fat: 25g, Fiber: 3g, Cholesterol: 80mg, Sodium: 500mg, Potassium: 600mg.

SERVINGS: 4   PREPPING TIME: 20 MIN   COOKING TIME: 45 MIN

SOUTZOUKAKIA

INGREDIENTS

For the Meatballs:
- 1 pound ground beef
- 1/2 pound ground pork
- 1 onion, grated
- 2 cloves garlic, minced
- 1/2 cup breadcrumbs
- 1 egg
- 1 teaspoon ground cumin
- Salt and pepper to taste

For the Tomato Sauce:
- 1 can (14 ounces) diced tomatoes
- 1/4 cup tomato paste
- 1/4 cup red wine
- 2 cloves garlic, minced
- 1 teaspoon ground cinnamon
- Salt and pepper to taste
- 2 tablespoons olive oil

DIRECTIONS

1. In a large bowl, combine all the meatball ingredients and mix well.
2. Shape the mixture into oblong meatballs.
3. In a skillet, heat the olive oil over medium-high heat. Brown the meatballs on all sides.
4. Remove the meatballs from the skillet and set them aside.
5. In the same skillet, add the minced garlic and sauté for a minute.
6. Stir in the diced tomatoes, tomato paste, red wine, ground cinnamon, salt, and pepper. Simmer for 15-20 minutes to thicken the sauce.
7. Return the meatballs to the skillet and simmer for an additional 10-15 minutes, or until the meatballs are cooked through and the sauce is flavorful.
8. Serve the Soutzoukakia hot with tomato sauce.

Nutritional Information (approximation per serving)*: Calories: 450, Protein: 30g, Carbohydrates: 15g, Fat: 30g, Fiber: 3g, Cholesterol: 120mg, Sodium: 650mg, Potassium: 600mg.

SERVINGS: 4   PREPPING TIME: 20 MIN   COOKING TIME: 10 MIN

SOUVLAKI

INGREDIENTS

1 pound lean beef or chicken, cut into cubes
4 whole wheat pita bread or flatbreads
1 red bell pepper, cut into strips
1 green bell pepper, cut into strips
1 red onion, cut into wedges
Juice of 1 lemon
2 cloves garlic, minced
2 tablespoons olive oil
1 teaspoon dried oregano
Salt and pepper to taste
Wooden skewers, soaked in water

DIRECTIONS

1. In a bowl, mix together the minced garlic, olive oil, lemon juice, dried oregano, salt, and pepper to prepare the marinade.
2. Thread the beef or chicken cubes onto the wooden skewers, alternating with the bell pepper strips and onion wedges. Brush the skewers with the marinade and let them marinate for at least 15 minutes. Preheat a grill or grill pan over medium-high heat.
3. Grill the skewers for about 5 minutes on each side, or until the meat is cooked and has grill marks.
4. Warm the whole wheat pita bread or flatbreads on the grill for a minute on each side.
5. Serve the souvlaki by placing a portion of the grilled meat and vegetables on each warm pita bread. Fold the pita bread around the filling and serve immediately.

SERVINGS: 4   PREPPING TIME: 15 MIN   COOKING TIME: 15 MIN

TIGANIA

INGREDIENTS

1 pound pork loin, cut into strips
2 cloves garlic, minced
1 teaspoon dried oregano
1/4 cup olive oil
Juice of 1 lemon
Salt and pepper to taste
Fresh parsley for garnish (optional)

DIRECTIONS

1. In a bowl, combine the minced garlic, dried oregano, olive oil, lemon juice, salt, and pepper.
2. Add the pork strips to the marinade and let them marinate for at least 15 minutes.
3. In a skillet, heat some olive oil over medium-high heat. Add the marinated pork strips and cook until they are browned and cooked through.
4. Serve the Tigania hot, garnished with fresh parsley if desired.

Nutritional Information (approximation per serving)*: Calories: 320, Protein: 25g, Carbohydrates: 30g, Fat: 12g, Fiber: 5g, Cholesterol: 60mg, Sodium: 350mg, Potassium: 500mg.
Nutritional Information (approximation per serving)*: Calories: 350, Protein: 30g, Carbohydrates: 3g, Fat: 25g, Fiber: 1g, Cholesterol: 75mg, Sodium: 350mg, Potassium: 400mg.

RICE, PASTA, AND GRAIN DISHES
A Taste of Ikarian Tradition

In Ikaria, the humble grains of rice, pasta, and other cereals are elevated to an art form. This chapter delves into the heart of Ikarian culinary tradition, where these simple ingredients are transformed into dishes brimming with flavor and nourishment.

Rice Dishes: The Comfort of Home
Rice in Ikaria is not just a side dish, but a star in its own right. Recipes like "Gemista" - rice-stuffed tomatoes and peppers, and "Spanakorizo" - vibrant spinach and rice concoction, are household staples. These dishes are more than just food; they are a representation of the island's emphasis on family and community, where meals are a time for gathering and sharing.

Pasta: Crafting Simple Perfection
Pasta in Ikaria is a testament to the art of simplicity. "Kritharaki" - orzo cooked with juicy tomatoes and fragrant herbs, and "Hilopites" - homemade pasta, often served with a light, savory sauce, exemplify how basic ingredients can be transformed into heartwarming meals. These pasta dishes, often enjoyed with family, encapsulate the spirit of Ikarian cuisine – simple, satisfying, and made with love.

Grains: A Link to the Past
Ikarian cuisine honors its ancient roots through its use of grains. Barley and wheat, staples of the past, are used in dishes like "Trahanas" - a rustic, comforting soup that is both nutritious and delicious. These grain-based recipes are a nod to the island's agricultural heritage, showcasing the time-honored practices that have sustained Ikarians for generations.

Nutritional Wisdom in Every Bite
The use of rice, pasta, and grains in Ikarian cuisine aligns with the island's philosophy of longevity and wellness. These dishes are often high in fiber, packed with nutrients, and prepared in ways that maximize their health benefits. They embody the Ikarian secret to a

long and healthy life – eating wholesome, natural foods that nourish both the body and soul.

A Celebration of Flavors

This chapter is a celebration of Ikarian culinary artistry, where the simplicity of rice, pasta, and grains is transformed into an array of dishes, each bursting with flavor. It's an invitation to explore the rich tapestry of tastes and textures that make Ikarian cuisine so unique and beloved.

Culinary Stories from the Island

Each recipe is a story - a tale of tradition, of families passing down recipes through generations, of communal gatherings, and of a deep-rooted connection to the land. These dishes are more than just sustenance; they are a celebration of Ikarian life and its enduring culinary heritage.

Cooking Tips and Techniques

For the perfect consistency in dishes like Kritharoto and Manestra, use a good stock and stir frequently to release the starches.

Fresh, local ingredients are key to enhancing the natural flavors of these dishes.

Health and Nutrition Information

Rice, pasta, and grain dishes provide essential carbohydrates and fibers, integral to a balanced diet. Incorporating vegetables, legumes, and lean proteins with these grains aligns with the Mediterranean and Blue Zone dietary principles, promoting health and longevity.

In conclusion, this chapter is a journey through the heart of Ikarian cuisine, where the simplest of ingredients are turned into extraordinary meals. It's a tribute to the island's culinary traditions and a reflection of its vibrant culture and way of life.

RECIPES

- **Hilopites:** Traditional Ikarian pasta, often homemade, served with a variety of sauces or simply with grated cheese and a drizzle of olive oil.
- **Kritharoto:** A risotto-like dish made with orzo (barley-shaped pasta), often cooked with a rich tomato sauce or seafood.
- **Makarounes:** Handmade pasta, typically served with a simple yet aromatic sauce, showcasing the island's rustic culinary style.
- **Manestra:** A comforting orzo dish, usually prepared with tomato sauce and a touch of cinnamon, bringing warmth to any meal.
- **Spanakorizo:** A classic spinach and rice dish, often cooked with herbs and lemon, offering a healthy and satisfying meal option.
- **Rizogalo:** Creamy rice pudding, a traditional dessert flavored with cinnamon and lemon zest, is loved for its simplicity and comfort.
- **Rizopita:** A unique rice pie, combining creamy rice with a flaky pastry crust, a fusion of traditional Ikarian flavors.

SERVINGS: 4   PREPPING TIME: 30 MIN   COOKING TIME: 10 MIN

HILOPITES

INGREDIENTS
2 cups all-purpose flour
2 large eggs
Water (as needed)
Salt to taste

DIRECTIONS
1. In a large mixing bowl, combine the flour and a pinch of salt.
2. Make a well in the center of the flour and crack the eggs into it.
3. Begin mixing the eggs into the flour with a fork or your hands.
4. Gradually add small amounts of water as needed to form a dough. Continue kneading until the dough is smooth and elastic. Roll out the dough on a floured surface until it's very thin, almost translucent. Let the rolled-out dough rest for about 10 minutes.
5. Cut the dough into small squares or diamonds, about 1 to 1.5 inches in size.
6. Allow the hilopites to dry for a few hours or overnight before cooking.
7. To cook, bring a pot of salted water to a boil. Add the hilopites and cook for about 2-3 minutes or until they float to the surface. Drain the hilopites and serve with your favorite sauce or in soups.

SERVINGS: 4   PREPPING TIME: 5 MIN   COOKING TIME: 20 MIN

KRITHAROTO

INGREDIENTS
1 cup orzo pasta
2 tablespoons olive oil
1 onion, chopped
2 cloves garlic, minced
1 can (14 ounces) diced tomatoes
2 cups chicken or vegetable broth
1 teaspoon dried oregano
Salt and pepper to taste
Grated Parmesan cheese for serving (optional)
Fresh parsley for garnish (optional)

DIRECTIONS
1. In a large skillet, heat the olive oil over medium heat. Add the chopped onion and sauté until translucent. Add the minced garlic and sauté for another minute until fragrant.
2. Stir in the orzo pasta and cook for a few minutes until it starts to brown.
3. Pour in the diced tomatoes, chicken or vegetable broth, dried oregano, salt, and pepper.
4. Cover the skillet and simmer for about 15-20 minutes, or until the orzo is cooked and the liquid is absorbed. Fluff the orzo with a fork and adjust the seasoning with salt and pepper as needed. Serve hot, garnished with grated Parmesan cheese and fresh parsley if desired.

Nutritional Information (approximation per serving)*: Calories: 150 (per 1 cup cooked), Protein: 6g, Fat: 1g, Carbohydrates: 30g, Fiber: 1g, Cholesterol: 50mg, Sodium: 10mg, Potassium: 40mg.
Nutritional Information (approximation per serving)*: Calories: 250, Protein: 6g, Carbohydrates: 45g, Fat: 5g, Fiber: 2g, Cholesterol: 0mg, Sodium: 400mg, Potassium: 250mg.

SERVINGS: 4   PREPPING TIME: 30 MIN   COOKING TIME: 5-10 MIN

MAKAROUNES

INGREDIENTS

2 cups all-purpose flour
2 large eggs
Water (as needed)
Salt to taste

DIRECTIONS

1. In a large mixing bowl, combine the flour and a pinch of salt.
2. Make a well in the center of the flour and crack the eggs into it. Begin mixing the eggs into the flour with a fork or your hands. Gradually add small amounts of water as needed to form a dough. Continue kneading until the dough is smooth and elastic.
3. Roll out the dough on a floured surface until it's very thin, almost translucent.
4. Let the rolled-out dough rest for about 10 minutes. Cut the dough into strips or shapes of your choice. Allow the makarounes to dry for a few hours or overnight before cooking.
5. To cook, bring a pot of salted water to a boil. Add the makarounes and cook for about 5-10 minutes or until they are tender.
6. Drain the makarounes and serve with your favorite sauce.

SERVINGS: 4   PREPPING TIME: 5 MIN   COOKING TIME: 30 MIN

RIZOGALO

INGREDIENTS

1/2 cup Arborio rice
4 cups whole milk
1/2 cup sugar
1 teaspoon vanilla extract
Ground cinnamon for garnish

DIRECTIONS

1. Rinse the rice under cold water and drain it.
2. In a saucepan, combine the rice and 2 cups of milk. Bring it to a boil over medium heat, then reduce the heat to low and simmer, stirring frequently until the rice is cooked and the mixture thickens (about 15-20 minutes).
3. Stir in the sugar and continue to cook for another 5-10 minutes until the sugar is dissolved and the pudding thickens further.
4. Remove the saucepan from heat and stir in the remaining 2 cups of milk and vanilla extract.
5. Allow the rice pudding to cool to room temperature, then refrigerate until chilled.
6. Serve the Rizogalo cold, garnished with ground cinnamon.

Nutritional Information (approximation per serving)*: Calories: 180 (per 1 cup cooked), Protein: 6g, Fat: 1g, Carbohydrates: 36g, Fiber: 2g, Cholesterol: 50mg, Sodium: 10mg, Potassium: 60mg.
Nutritional Information (approximation per serving)*: Calories 300, Protein 7g, Carbohydrates 57g, Fat 5g, Fiber 0g, Cholesterol 20mg, Sodium 100mg, Potassium 270mg.

SERVINGS: 4　　　PREPPING TIME: 10 MIN　　　COOKING TIME: 30 MIN

MANESTRA

INGREDIENTS

1 cup orzo pasta
1 onion, chopped
2 cloves garlic, minced
2 tablespoons olive oil
1 can (14 ounces) diced tomatoes
1/2 cup tomato sauce
1 teaspoon dried oregano
Salt and pepper to taste
1/2 pound ground meat (beef, lamb, or chicken) - optional
Grated Parmesan cheese for serving (optional)
Fresh parsley for garnish (optional)

DIRECTIONS

1. In a large skillet, heat the olive oil over medium heat. If using meat, add the ground meat and cook until browned. Remove any excess fat.
2. Add the chopped onion and sauté until translucent.
3. Add the minced garlic and sauté for another minute until fragrant.
4. Stir in the diced tomatoes, tomato sauce, dried oregano, salt, and pepper. If you're not using meat, you can add the orzo directly at this stage.
5. Simmer the sauce for about 10 minutes to let the flavors meld.
6. If you're using meat, return the cooked meat to the skillet.
7. Stir in the orzo pasta and add enough water to cover the pasta. Bring it to a boil.
8. Reduce the heat, cover the skillet, and simmer for about 15-20 minutes, or until the orzo is cooked and the sauce has thickened.
9. Adjust the seasoning with salt and pepper as needed.
10. Serve hot, garnished with grated Parmesan cheese and fresh parsley if desired.

Nutritional Information (approximation per serving)*: Calories: 350 (without meat) - 450 (with meat), Protein: 10g (without meat) - 20g (with meat), Carbohydrates: 60g, Fat: 10g (without meat) - 20g (with meat), Fiber: 4g, Cholesterol: 20mg (without meat) - 50mg (with meat), Sodium: 400mg (without meat) - 600mg (with meat), Potassium: 500mg (without meat) - 700mg (with meat).

SERVINGS: 4 **PREPPING TIME: 15 MIN** **COOKING TIME: 25 MIN**

SPANAKORIZO

INGREDIENTS

1 cup long-grain rice
2 tablespoons extra virgin olive oil
1 small onion, finely chopped
2 cloves garlic, minced
1 bunch fresh spinach, chopped
1/4 cup fresh dill, chopped
1/4 cup fresh parsley, chopped
1 lemon, zest and juice
2 cups vegetable broth
Salt and pepper to taste
Crumbled feta cheese for garnish (optional)

DIRECTIONS

1. Rinse the rice under cold water and drain.
2. In a large skillet, heat the olive oil over medium heat. Add the chopped onion and sauté until translucent.
3. Add the minced garlic and sauté for another minute until fragrant.
4. Add the chopped spinach, dill, and parsley to the skillet. Cook for a few minutes until the spinach wilts.
5. Stir in the rice and cook for 1-2 minutes, stirring constantly.
6. Add the lemon zest, lemon juice, vegetable broth, salt, and pepper. Stir well.
7. Bring the mixture to a boil, then reduce the heat to low, cover, and simmer for 15-20 minutes, or until the rice is tender and has absorbed the liquid.
8. Fluff the Spanakorizo with a fork and garnish with crumbled feta cheese if desired before serving.

Nutritional Information (approximation per serving)*: Calories: 220, Protein: 4g, Carbohydrates: 41g, Fat: 5g, Fiber: 2g, Cholesterol: 0mg, Sodium: 450mg, Potassium: 280mg.

SERVINGS: 8   PREPPING TIME: 15 MIN   COOKING TIME: 1 HOUR

RIZOPITA

INGREDIENTS

- 1 cup Arborio rice
- 4 cups water
- 1/2 cup sugar
- 2 tablespoons unsalted butter
- 1/2 teaspoon ground cinnamon
- 1/4 teaspoon salt
- 1 teaspoon vanilla extract
- Zest of 1 orange
- 1/2 cup raisins
- 1/4 cup chopped walnuts
- 2 large eggs
- Phyllo pastry sheets (about 8-10 sheets)
- Cooking spray or melted butter for brushing the phyllo sheets
- Powdered sugar for dusting (optional)

DIRECTIONS

1. In a large pot, combine the Arborio rice and water. Bring it to a boil, then reduce the heat to low and simmer for about 15-20 minutes, or until the rice is cooked and most of the water is absorbed. Remove from heat and let it cool.
2. Preheat your oven to 350°F (175°C) and grease a 9x9-inch (23x23 cm) baking dish.
3. In a saucepan, melt the unsalted butter over low heat. Stir in the sugar, ground cinnamon, and salt until well combined.
4. Remove the saucepan from heat and stir in the vanilla extract, orange zest, raisins, and chopped walnuts.
5. Beat the eggs separately and gradually add them to the sugar mixture, stirring constantly.
6. Combine the cooked rice with the sugar mixture, mixing thoroughly.
7. Layer half of the phyllo pastry sheets in the bottom of the greased baking dish, brushing each sheet with cooking spray or melted butter.
8. Pour the rice mixture over the phyllo sheets.
9. Layer the remaining phyllo pastry sheets on top, brushing each sheet with cooking spray or melted butter.
10. Score the top of the pie with a sharp knife into serving portions.
11. Bake in the preheated oven for about 30-40 minutes, or until the phyllo is golden brown and crispy.
12. Remove from the oven and allow it to cool slightly.
13. Dust the top with powdered sugar if desired.
14. Serve warm or at room temperature.

Nutritional Information (approximation per serving)*: Calories: 290, Protein: 5g, Carbohydrates: 50g, Fat: 8g, Fiber: 1g, Cholesterol: 50mg, Sodium: 190mg, Potassium: 140mg.

SEAFOOD DISHES
The Essence of the Aegean Sea

The island of Ikaria, embraced by the Aegean Sea, is a place where seafood is not just a part of the diet but a way of life. In this chapter, we dive deep into the ocean's bounty, exploring the traditional and innovative ways Ikarians prepare seafood.

Seafood: A Daily Ritual
In Ikaria, the proximity to the sea means fresh seafood is a daily affair. From the simple "Grilled Octopus" that captures the essence of the sea, to the more intricate "Psarosoupa" - a rich and hearty fish soup, each dish tells a story of the island's love affair with the ocean.

Octopus: A Delicacy of the Deep
Octopus is a beloved ingredient in Ikarian cuisine. Dishes like "Octopus Stifado" with its slow-cooked, tender pieces in a rich tomato sauce, and "Xtapodi Ksidato" - a tangy, vinegar-marinated octopus, are not just meals but a celebration of the island's fishing traditions.

Fish: The Heart of Ikarian Cuisine
Fish, the heart of Ikarian cuisine, is prepared in countless ways, each reflecting the island's culinary ingenuity. "Psari Plaki" - baked fish with tomatoes and herbs, exemplifies the island's knack for enhancing the natural flavors of the sea. "Psari Sto Fourno me Ladolemono" - fish baked with a fragrant lemon-olive oil sauce, is another testament to the island's simple yet flavorful approach to cooking.

Sardines: A Staple of Ikarian Diets
Sardines, a staple in the Ikarian diet, are not only delicious but also embody the island's philosophy of healthy living. "Sardeles Kefalonia" - fried sardines, and "Sardeles Pastes" - salted sardines, are traditional preparations that highlight this humble fish's nutritional value.

Nutrition from the Sea
Seafood dishes in Ikaria are not just about taste but also about health. Rich in omega-3 fatty acids, minerals, and vitamins, these dishes are integral to the Ikarian diet, contributing to the longevity and wellness of its people.

Stories from the Aegean
Behind every seafood dish in Ikaria are stories of early morning fishing trips, family gatherings by the seaside, and age-old cooking techniques passed down through generations. These recipes are a window into the island's soul, offering a taste of life by the Aegean Sea.

Cooking Tips and Techniques
Freshness is key for seafood dishes. The less time between the sea and the table, the better the flavor.
Simple seasonings like lemon, olive oil, and fresh herbs enhance the natural taste of seafood without overpowering it.

Health and Nutrition Information
Seafood is a cornerstone of both the Mediterranean and Blue Zone diets, rich in omega-3 fatty acids, lean proteins, and essential nutrients. Regular consumption of seafood, as part of a balanced diet, is linked to improved heart health and longevity.

In conclusion, in essence, this chapter is more than a collection of seafood recipes; it's an ode to the Aegean Sea and its gifts. It's a journey into the heart of Ikarian cuisine, where the sea's treasures are turned into culinary masterpieces that capture the spirit of the island.

RECIPES

- **Astakos:** A luxurious lobster dish, often grilled or cooked in a flavorful broth, epitomizing the island's love for fresh, quality seafood.
- **Atherina:** Small, silvery fish, typically fried until crisp, offering a delightful snack or appetizer.
- **Fournisto:** Baked fish, marinated with herbs and lemon, showcasing the simplicity of Greek cooking.
- **Fried Marides:** Tiny, crispy fried fish, enjoyed as a tasty, quick bite.
- **Fried Sardines:** A classic Greek preparation, highlighting the richness of sardines with a crispy exterior.
- **Gouna:** Sun-dried and grilled mackerel, a unique traditional method of preserving fish.
- **Kakavia:** A rich fisherman's soup, brimming with various kinds of fish and seasoned with fresh herbs.
- **Kalamarakia:** Tender squid, either grilled or fried, often served with a garlic lemon sauce.
- **Marida Skaras:** Grilled white bait, a simple yet delicious treat from the sea.
- **Octopus Krasato:** Octopus cooked in red wine, a dish that melds the flavors of the sea with the earthiness of wine.
- **Octopus Stifado:** A stew combining octopus with onions and a rich tomato sauce, infused with spices.
- **Psari Plaki:** A traditional baked fish dish with tomatoes, onions, and plenty of olive oil.
- **Psari Sto Fourno me Ladolemono:** Oven-baked fish finished with a classic Greek sauce of lemon and olive oil.
- **Sardeles Kefalonia:** Sardines prepared in the style of Kefalonia, often featuring a tomato-based sauce.
- **Sardeles Pastes:** Salted and cured sardines, a traditional method of preserving the catch.
- **Xtapodi Ksidato:** Tender octopus in a tangy vinegar sauce, a perfect meze for ouzo.

SERVINGS: 2 PREPPING TIME: 15 MIN COOKING TIME: 20 MIN

ASTAKOS

INGREDIENTS

2 lobsters (about 1 to 1.5 pounds each)
4 cloves garlic, minced
Juice of 2 lemons
1/4 cup olive oil
Salt and pepper to taste
Fresh parsley for garnish

DIRECTIONS

1. Preheat your grill or broiler.
2. Split the lobsters in half lengthwise.
3. In a small bowl, combine the minced garlic, lemon juice, olive oil, salt, and pepper.
4. Brush the lobster halves generously with the garlic and lemon mixture.
5. Grill or broil the lobsters for about 10 minutes on each side, or until the meat is opaque and cooked through.
6. Garnish with fresh parsley and serve hot.

SERVINGS: 4 PREPPING TIME: 15 MIN COOKING TIME: 10 MIN

ATHERINA

INGREDIENTS

1 pound fresh smelts, cleaned and gutted
1 cup all-purpose flour
Salt and pepper to taste
Vegetable oil for frying
Lemon wedges for serving

DIRECTIONS

1. In a deep skillet or frying pan, heat enough vegetable oil to cover the smelts over medium-high heat.
2. In a shallow dish, combine the flour, salt, and pepper.
3. Dredge each smelt in the flour mixture, ensuring they are coated evenly.
4. Carefully place the coated smelts into the hot oil and fry for about 2-3 minutes on each side, or until they are golden brown and crispy.
5. Remove the fried smelts from the oil and place them on paper towels to drain excess oil. Serve hot with lemon wedges for squeezing.

Nutritional Information (approximation per serving)*: Calories: 350, Protein: 40g, Carbohydrates: 4g, Fat: 20g, Fiber: 0g, Cholesterol: 150mg, Sodium: 300mg, Potassium: 400mg.
Nutritional Information (approximation per serving)*: Calories: 250, Protein: 20g, Carbohydrates: 20g, Fat: 10g, Fiber: 1g, Cholesterol: 50mg, Sodium: 300mg, Potassium: 200mg.

SERVINGS: 4   PREPPING TIME: 15 MIN   COOKING TIME: 30 MIN

FOURNISTO

INGREDIENTS

4 fish fillets (such as cod, snapper, or sea bass)
2 tomatoes, thinly sliced
1 onion, thinly sliced
2 cloves garlic, minced
1 lemon, sliced
1/4 cup olive oil
1/2 cup white wine
1 tablespoon fresh oregano, chopped
Salt and pepper to taste
Fresh parsley, chopped for garnish

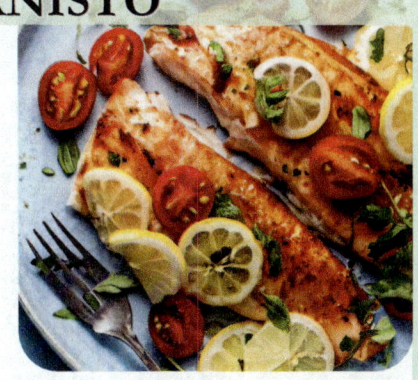

DIRECTIONS

1. Preheat the oven to 200°C (400°F).
2. Place the fish fillets in a baking dish. Season with salt and pepper.
3. Arrange tomato, onion, and lemon slices over and around the fish.
4. Sprinkle minced garlic and oregano on top.
5. Drizzle olive oil and white wine over the fish.
6. Bake in the preheated oven for 25-30 minutes, or until the fish flakes easily with a fork.
7. Garnish with fresh parsley before serving.

SERVINGS: 4   PREPPING TIME: 15 MIN   COOKING TIME: 10 MIN

FRIED MARIDES

INGREDIENTS

1 pound fresh whitebait (marides), cleaned and gutted
1 cup all-purpose flour
Salt and pepper to taste
Vegetable oil for frying
Lemon wedges for serving

DIRECTIONS

1. In a deep skillet or frying pan, heat enough vegetable oil to cover the whitebait over medium-high heat.
2. In a shallow dish, combine the flour, salt, and pepper.
3. Dredge each whitebait in the flour mixture, ensuring they are coated evenly.
4. Carefully place the coated whitebait into the hot oil and fry for about 2-3 minutes on each side, or until they are golden brown and crispy.
5. Remove the fried whitebait from the oil and place them on paper towels to drain excess oil.
6. Serve hot with lemon wedges for squeezing.

Nutritional Information (approximation per serving)*: Calories: 280, Protein: 25g, Carbohydrates: 6g, Fat: 15g, Fiber: 1g, Cholesterol: 60mg, Sodium: 100mg, Potassium: 600mg.
Nutritional Information (approximation per serving)*: Calories: 200, Protein: 15g, Carbohydrates: 15g, Fat: 8g, Fiber: 1g, Cholesterol: 30mg, Sodium: 250mg, Potassium: 150mg.

SERVINGS: 4   PREPPING TIME: 15 MIN   COOKING TIME: 10 MIN

FRIED SARDINES

INGREDIENTS

1 pound fresh sardines, cleaned and gutted
1 cup all-purpose flour
Salt and pepper to taste
Vegetable oil for frying
Lemon wedges for serving

DIRECTIONS

1. In a deep skillet or frying pan, heat enough vegetable oil to cover the sardines over medium-high heat.
2. In a shallow dish, combine the flour, salt, and pepper.
3. Dredge each sardine in the flour mixture, ensuring they are coated evenly.
4. Carefully place the coated sardines into the hot oil and fry for about 2-3 minutes on each side, or until they are golden brown and crispy.
5. Remove the fried sardines from the oil and place them on paper towels to drain excess oil. Serve hot with lemon wedges for squeezing.

SERVINGS: 4   PREPPING TIME: 15 MIN   COOKING TIME: 15 MIN (PLUS DRYING TIME)

GOUNA

INGREDIENTS

4 fresh mackerel, cleaned and gutted
1/2 cup coarse sea salt
Lemon wedges for serving
Olive oil (optional)g

DIRECTIONS

1. Rinse the mackerel and pat them dry with paper towels.
2. Rub each mackerel generously with coarse sea salt, ensuring it covers the entire surface.
3. Place the salted mackerel on a wire rack or a tray and let them air-dry in a cool, dry place for about 2-3 days until they become firm. Preheat your grill or broiler.
4. Grill or broil the salted mackerel for about 5-7 minutes on each side, or until they are cooked and slightly crispy.
5. Serve hot with lemon wedges and a drizzle of olive oil if desired.

Nutritional Information (approximation per serving)*: Calories: 220, Protein: 18g, Carbohydrates: 15g, Fat: 10g, Fiber: 1g, Cholesterol: 40mg, Sodium: 250mg, Potassium: 200mg.
Nutritional Information (approximation per serving)*: Calories: 150, Protein: 20g, Carbohydrates: 0g, Fat: 7g, Fiber: 0g, Cholesterol: 40mg.

SERVINGS: 6   PREPPING TIME: 20 MIN   COOKING TIME: 45 MIN

KAKAVIA

INGREDIENTS

1 pound mixed fish (such as cod, shrimp, and mussels), cleaned and cut into chunks
1 onion, chopped
2 cloves garlic, minced
2 carrots, chopped
2 celery stalks, chopped
2 potatoes, peeled and diced
1/2 cup olive oil
1 can (14 ounces) diced tomatoes
1/4 cup white wine (optional)
6 cups water
2 bay leaves
Salt and pepper to taste
Fresh parsley for garnish
Lemon wedges for serving

DIRECTIONS

1. In a large pot, heat the olive oil over medium heat. Add the chopped onion and garlic and sauté until translucent.
2. Add the carrots, celery, and potatoes to the pot and sauté for a few minutes.
3. Pour in the white wine and let it simmer for a couple of minutes.
4. Add the diced tomatoes, bay leaves, salt, and pepper. Stir well.
5. Pour in the water and bring the soup to a boil.
6. Reduce the heat and let the soup simmer for about 30 minutes or until the vegetables are tender.
7. Add the mixed fish chunks to the pot and simmer for an additional 10-15 minutes, or until the fish is cooked.
8. Remove the bay leaves.
9. Serve hot, garnished with fresh parsley and lemon wedges.

Nutritional Information (approximation per serving)*: Calories: 250, Protein: 20g, Carbohydrates: 15g, Fat: 12g, Fiber: 3g, Cholesterol: 40mg, Sodium: 600mg, Potassium: 700mg.

SERVINGS: 4 PREPPING TIME: 15 MIN COOKING TIME: 10 MIN

MARIDA SKARAS

INGREDIENTS

1 pound fresh smelt, cleaned and gutted
1/4 cup olive oil
Juice of 1 lemon
2 cloves garlic, minced
1 teaspoon dried oregano
Salt and pepper to taste
Lemon wedges for serving

DIRECTIONS

1. Preheat your grill or broiler.
2. In a bowl, combine the olive oil, lemon juice, minced garlic, dried oregano, salt, and pepper.
3. Brush the cleaned smelt with the olive oil mixture, ensuring they are coated evenly.
4. Grill or broil the smelt for about 3-4 minutes on each side, or until they are cooked through and have grill marks.
5. Remove from heat and serve hot with lemon wedges.

SERVINGS: 4 PREPPING TIME: 15 MIN COOKING TIME: 1 HOUR 30 MIN

OCTOPUS KRASATO

INGREDIENTS

2 pounds octopus, cleaned and cut into pieces
1 onion, chopped
2 cloves garlic, minced
1 cup red wine
1/4 cup olive oil
1 can (14 ounces) diced tomatoes
1 teaspoon dried oregano
Salt and pepper to taste
Fresh parsley for garnish
Lemon wedges for serving

DIRECTIONS

1. In a deep pot, heat the olive oil over medium heat. Add the chopped onion and minced garlic and sauté until translucent.
2. Add the octopus pieces to the pot and sauté for about 10 minutes, allowing them to release their liquid and then evaporate. Pour in the red wine and let it simmer for a few minutes. Add the diced tomatoes, dried oregano, salt, and pepper. Stir well.
3. Reduce the heat, cover, and simmer for about 1 hour or until the octopus is tender.
4. Remove the lid and continue simmering for an additional 15-20 minutes to thicken the sauce. Serve hot, garnished with fresh parsley and lemon wedges.

Nutritional Information (approximation per serving)*: Calories: 250, Protein: 20g, Carbohydrates: 0g, Fat: 18g, Fiber: 0g, Cholesterol: 60mg, Sodium: 150mg, Potassium: 180mg.
Nutritional Information (approximation per serving)*: Calories: 280, Protein: 25g, Carbohydrates: 7g, Fat: 10g, Fiber: 2g, Cholesterol: 70mg, Sodium: 350mg, Potassium: 600mg.

SERVINGS: 4   PREPPING TIME: 15 MIN   COOKING TIME: 10 MIN

KALAMARAKIA

INGREDIENTS

1 pound fresh calamari rings
1 cup all-purpose flour
Salt and pepper to taste
Vegetable oil for frying
Lemon wedges for serving
Tzatziki sauce for dipping (optional)

DIRECTIONS

1. In a deep skillet or frying pan, heat enough vegetable oil to cover the calamari rings over medium-high heat.
2. In a shallow dish, combine the flour, salt, and pepper.
3. Dredge each calamari ring in the flour mixture, ensuring they are coated evenly.
4. Carefully place the coated calamari rings into the hot oil and fry for about 2-3 minutes until they are golden brown and crispy.
5. Remove the fried calamari from the oil and place them on paper towels to drain excess oil.
6. Serve hot with lemon wedges and tzatziki sauce for dipping if desired.

SERVINGS: 4   PREPPING TIME: 20 MIN   COOKING TIME: 60 MIN

OCTOPUS STIFADO

INGREDIENTS

1 kg octopus, cleaned and cut into pieces
2 large onions, sliced
4 garlic cloves, minced
1 cup red wine
1/2 cup olive oil
2 cups tomato sauce
1 cinnamon stick
4 allspice berries
1 bay leaf
Salt and pepper to taste

DIRECTIONS

1. Rinse the octopus under cold water and place in a large pot. Cover and cook over medium heat for about 20 minutes, or until octopus is tender.
2. Heat olive oil in a separate pan and sauté onions and garlic until translucent.
3. Add the cooked octopus to the pan with onions and garlic. Pour in red wine and simmer for 10 minutes.
4. Add tomato sauce, cinnamon stick, allspice berries, bay leaf, salt, and pepper. Simmer for another 30 minutes.
5. Remove cinnamon stick, allspice berries, and bay leaf before serving.
6. Serve hot with crusty bread or over rice.

Nutritional Information (approximation per serving)*: Calories: 220, Protein: 20g, Carbohydrates: 15g, Fat: 8g, Fiber: 1g, Cholesterol: 30mg, Sodium: 250mg, Potassium: 200mg.

Nutritional Information (approximation per serving)*: Calories: 350, Protein: 40g, Carbohydrates: 15g, Fat: 15g, Fiber: 2g, Cholesterol: 75mg, Sodium: 500mg, Potassium: 750mg.

SERVINGS: 4   PREPPING TIME: 15 MIN   COOKING TIME: 25 MIN

PSARI STO FOURNO ME LADOLEMONO

INGREDIENTS

4 medium-sized whole fish (e.g., sea bream, trout), cleaned and scaled
2 lemons, juiced
1/2 cup olive oil
4 garlic cloves, minced
1 tablespoon dried oregano
Salt and pepper to taste
Lemon slices and fresh parsley for garnish

Ladolemono Sauce:
1/2 cup olive oil
1/4 cup lemon juice
1 teaspoon Dijon mustard
1 garlic clove, minced
Salt and pepper to taste

DIRECTIONS

1. Preheat the oven to 200°C (400°F).
2. In a bowl, mix lemon juice, olive oil, minced garlic, oregano, salt, and pepper. Rub this mixture inside and outside of the fish.
3. Place the fish in a baking dish and bake for 20-25 minutes, or until the fish is cooked through and flakes easily with a fork.
4. For the ladolemono sauce, whisk together olive oil, lemon juice, Dijon mustard, minced garlic, salt, and pepper in a small bowl.
5. Serve the fish hot, drizzled with the ladolemono sauce and garnished with lemon slices and fresh parsley.

Nutritional Information (approximation per serving)*: Calories: 380, Protein: 40g, Carbohydrates: 3g, Fat: 24g, Fiber: 1g, Cholesterol: 60mg, Sodium: 200mg, Potassium: 600mg.

SERVINGS: 4   PREPPING TIME: 15 MIN   COOKING TIME: 40 MIN

PSARI PLAKI

INGREDIENTS

- 4 medium-sized whole fish (e.g., snapper, sea bass), cleaned and scaled
- 2 large onions, thinly sliced
- 4 garlic cloves, minced
- 2 large tomatoes, diced
- 1/2 cup olive oil
- 1/2 cup white wine
- 1/4 cup fresh parsley, chopped
- 1 tablespoon dried oregano
- Salt and pepper to taste
- Lemon slices for garnish

DIRECTIONS

1. Preheat the oven to 180°C (350°F).
2. Arrange onion slices in the bottom of a baking dish. Place fish on top of the onions.
3. In a bowl, mix garlic, tomatoes, olive oil, white wine, parsley, oregano, salt, and pepper. Pour this mixture over the fish.
4. Cover with aluminum foil and bake in the preheated oven for 30 minutes.
5. Remove the foil and bake for an additional 10 minutes or until the fish is cooked through and slightly browned.
6. Garnish with lemon slices and serve with a side of steamed vegetables or rice.

SERVINGS: 4   PREPPING TIME: 10 MIN   COOKING TIME: 15 MIN

SARDELES KEFALONIA

INGREDIENTS

- 500g fresh sardines, cleaned and heads removed
- 1 cup all-purpose flour
- 1/2 cup olive oil for frying
- Salt to taste
- Lemon wedges for serving

DIRECTIONS

1. Rinse the sardines and pat them dry with paper towels.
2. Season the sardines with salt and lightly coat them with flour.
3. Heat olive oil in a frying pan over medium-high heat.
4. Fry the sardines in batches for 2-3 minutes on each side, or until golden brown and crispy. Remove the sardines from the pan and drain on paper towels.
5. Serve hot with lemon wedges.

Nutritional Information (approximation per serving)*: Calories: 400, Protein: 45g, Carbohydrates: 10g, Fat: 20g, Fiber: 2g, Cholesterol: 80mg, Sodium: 300mg, Potassium: 800mg.
Nutritional Information (approximation per serving)*: Calories: 290, Protein: 25g, Carbohydrates: 12g, Fat: 15g, Fiber: 1g, Cholesterol: 85mg, Sodium: 250mg, Potassium: 400mg.

SERVINGS: 4   PREPPING TIME: 15 MIN (PLUS CURING TIME)   COOKING TIME: 0 MIN

SARDELES PASTES

INGREDIENTS

500g fresh sardines, cleaned and heads removed
Coarse sea salt
Olive oil, for storage
Lemon wedges and chopped parsley for serving

DIRECTIONS

1. Rinse the sardines and pat them dry.
2. Layer the sardines in a container, generously sprinkling each layer with coarse sea salt.
3. Cover the container and refrigerate for at least 48 hours to cure the sardines.
4. After curing, rinse the sardines under cold water to remove excess salt.
5. Pat the sardines dry and layer them in a clean jar, covering each layer with olive oil.
6. Store the jar in the refrigerator.
7. Serve the sardines with lemon wedges and chopped parsley.

SERVINGS: 4   PREPPING TIME: 20 MIN   COOKING TIME: 60 MIN

XTAPODI KSIDATO

INGREDIENTS

1 kg octopus, cleaned
1 cup red wine vinegar
1/2 cup olive oil
2 bay leaves
1 teaspoon whole peppercorns
1 large onion, quartered
2 cloves garlic, minced
Salt to taste
Fresh parsley, chopped for garnish

DIRECTIONS

1. Place the octopus in a large pot and cover it with water. Bring to a boil, then reduce heat and simmer for about 45 minutes to 1 hour, or until the octopus is tender.
2. Drain the octopus and cut it into bite-sized pieces.
3. In a large bowl, mix red wine vinegar, olive oil, bay leaves, peppercorns, onion, garlic, and salt.
4. Add the cooked octopus to the vinegar mixture and let it marinate for at least 2 hours in the refrigerator. Before serving, remove the bay leaves and onion quarters.
5. Serve the octopus chilled, garnished with fresh parsley.

Nutritional Information (approximation per serving)*: Calories: 210, Protein: 20g, Carbohydrates: 0g, Fat: 14g, Fiber: 0g, Cholesterol: 60mg, Sodium: 1500mg, Potassium: 350mg.
Nutritional Information (approximation per serving)*: Calories: 330, Protein: 35g, Carbohydrates: 9g, Fat: 18g, Fiber: 1g, Cholesterol: 75mg, Sodium: 500mg, Potassium: 750mg.

SOUPS AND LEGUMES
A Warm Embrace from Ikarian Kitchens

In the heart of the Mediterranean, Ikaria's culinary landscape is rich with comforting soups and nutritious legumes. This chapter is a warm invitation into the cozy kitchens of Ikaria, where bowls of soul-satisfying soups and legumes speak of tradition, health, and the island's natural bounty.

The Art of Ikarian Soups
Soup in Ikaria is not just a dish; it's a ritual, a testament to the island's love for wholesome, heartening meals. "Fakes Soupa" - a traditional lentil soup, embodies the simplicity and nutritive value of Ikarian cuisine. Its humble ingredients, slow-cooked to perfection, create a dish that is both comforting and nourishing.

Fasolada: The Ikarian Comfort Food
"Fasolada" - Ikarian bean soup, is more than just a staple; it's a culinary heritage. This soup, with its rich blend of beans, vegetables, and herbs, is a classic example of how Ikarian cuisine transforms simple ingredients into a feast for the senses.

Gigantes Plaki: The Giant of Flavor
Ikaria's love for legumes is showcased in "Gigantes Plaki" - baked giant beans. This dish, with its hearty beans and flavorful tomato sauce, is a testament to the island's ability to create substantial and satisfying meals that are also healthful.

The Nutritional Powerhouse
Legumes and soups in Ikaria are not just about flavor. They are a cornerstone of the Ikarian diet, known for its health benefits and longevity-boosting properties. Rich in fiber, protein, and essential nutrients, these dishes are key to the islanders' famed health and longevity.

Ikarian Lifestyle: Slow Cooking, Shared Meals
In Ikaria, cooking is slow, and meals are meant to be shared. Soups and legumes are often cooked in large quantities, simmering for hours, their aromas filling the air, signifying a meal shared with family and friends. This communal aspect of Ikarian cooking is as nourishing for the soul as the food is for the body.

A Journey Through Flavor and Health
Each recipe in this chapter is a journey through the flavors and healthful eating habits of Ikaria. From the soothing "Kolokithosoupa" - a velvety zucchini soup, to the robust "Ikarian Lentil Soup," these dishes are a window into the soulful, health-conscious Ikarian way of life.

Cooking Tips and Techniques
Slow cooking is key to developing the flavors in these soups and legume dishes.
Use fresh herbs and vegetables for the best taste and nutritional benefits.
Don't rush the preparation of legumes; proper soaking and cooking ensure the perfect texture and digestibility.

Health and Nutrition Information
This chapter highlights the nutritional powerhouse of legumes and vegetables. Rich in fiber, protein, and essential nutrients, these dishes are integral to the heart-healthy and longevity-promoting aspects of the Mediterranean diet. They provide energy, aid in digestion, and are a great source of plant-based nutrition.

In conclusion
This chapter is more than just a compilation of recipes; it's a celebration of Ikaria's culinary traditions, where soups and legumes are a daily homage to the island's commitment to health, longevity, and the joy of shared meals.

RECIPES

- **Fakes Soupa:** A traditional Ikarian lentil soup, rich in flavor and nutrients, perfect for a cozy night.
- **Fasolada:** A classic bean soup, often considered the national dish of Greece, embodying simplicity and taste.
- **Gigantes Plaki:** Baked giant beans in a savory tomato sauce, a dish that's both hearty and delicious.
- **Kolokithosoupa:** A creamy zucchini soup that's light yet satisfying, embodying the freshness of garden vegetables.
- **Louvana:** A unique and flavorful pea soup, hailing from the culinary traditions of Ikaria.
- **Psarosoupa:** A traditional fish soup, combining a variety of seafood with a rich, aromatic broth.
- **Revithia:** A chickpea soup that's both simple and packed with flavor, showcasing the versatility of chickpeas.

SERVINGS: 6   PREPPING TIME: 10 MIN (PLUS OVERNIGHT SOAKING)   COOKING TIME: 90 MIN

GIGANTES PLAKI

INGREDIENTS

1 cup dried gigantes beans (or large lima beans), soaked overnight and drained
1 large onion, finely chopped
2 cloves garlic, minced
1 can (400g) diced tomatoes
1/4 cup olive oil
1 tablespoon tomato paste
1 teaspoon dried oregano
1/2 teaspoon smoked paprika
2 bay leaves
Salt and pepper to taste
Fresh parsley, chopped for garnish

DIRECTIONS

1. Preheat oven to 175°C (350°F).
2. In a large pot, cover the soaked beans with water and bring to a boil. Reduce heat and simmer for 30-40 minutes until slightly tender.
3. In a skillet, heat olive oil and sauté onion and garlic until translucent.
4. Add tomatoes, tomato paste, oregano, paprika, bay leaves, salt, and pepper to the skillet. Cook for 5 minutes.
5. Drain the beans and mix them with the tomato sauce. Transfer to a baking dish.
6. Cover with foil and bake for 60 minutes. Remove foil and bake for another 30 minutes until beans are tender and the top is caramelized.
7. Garnish with chopped parsley before serving.

Nutritional Information (approximation per serving)*: Calories: 230, Protein: 12g, Carbohydrates: 40g, Fat: 6g, Fiber: 10g, Cholesterol: 0mg, Sodium: 200mg, Potassium: 800mg.

SERVINGS: 6 PREPPING TIME: 10 MIN (PLUS OVERNIGHT SOAKING) COOKING TIME: 60 MIN

FASOLADA

INGREDIENTS

1 cup white beans (like navy or cannellini), soaked overnight and drained
1 large onion, chopped
2 carrots, diced
2 celery stalks, diced
3 garlic cloves, minced
1 can (400g) diced tomatoes
6 cups vegetable broth
1/4 cup olive oil
1 teaspoon dried oregano
Salt and pepper to taste
Parsley, chopped for garnish

DIRECTIONS

1. In a large pot, heat olive oil over medium heat. Add onions, carrots, celery, and garlic. Sauté until softened.
2. Add soaked and drained beans, diced tomatoes, vegetable broth, oregano, salt, and pepper.
3. Bring to a boil, then reduce heat and simmer for about 1 hour, or until beans are tender. Adjust seasoning as needed. Serve hot, garnished with chopped parsley.

SERVINGS: 4 PREPPING TIME: 15 MIN COOKING TIME: 30 MIN

KOLOKITHOSOUPA

INGREDIENTS

4 medium zucchinis, chopped
1 large potato, peeled and diced
1 large onion, chopped
2 cloves garlic, minced
5 cups vegetable broth
1/4 cup olive oil
1 teaspoon dried dill
Salt and pepper to taste
Lemon juice to taste
Grated kefalotyri or parmesan cheese for serving (optional)

DIRECTIONS

1. In a large pot, heat olive oil over medium heat. Add onions and garlic, and sauté until translucent. Add chopped zucchini and potato, and cook for 5 minutes.
2. Pour in vegetable broth and bring to a boil. Reduce heat, add dill, salt, and pepper, and simmer for about 20-25 minutes, or until vegetables are tender.
3. Use an immersion blender to puree the soup until smooth.
4. Adjust seasoning and add lemon juice to taste. Serve hot, topped with grated cheese if desired.

Nutritional Information (approximation per serving)*: Calories: 200, Protein: 10g, Carbohydrates: 30g, Fat: 5g, Fiber: 8g, Cholesterol: 0mg, Sodium: 300mg, Potassium: 700mg.
Nutritional Information (approximation per serving)*: Calories: 180, Protein: 4g, Carbohydrates: 20g, Fat: 10g, Fiber: 4g, Cholesterol: 0mg, Sodium: 400mg, Potassium: 650mg.

SERVINGS: 6   PREPPING TIME: 15 MIN   COOKING TIME: 45 MIN

FAKES SOUPA

INGREDIENTS

1 cup dried lentils, rinsed and drained
1 large onion, chopped
2 carrots, diced
2 stalks celery, diced
3 cloves garlic, minced
1 can (400g) diced tomatoes
6 cups vegetable broth
1/4 cup olive oil
1 teaspoon dried oregano
1 teaspoon smoked paprika
Salt and pepper to taste
2 tablespoons red wine vinegar
Fresh parsley, chopped for garnish

DIRECTIONS

1. In a large pot, heat olive oil over medium heat. Add onions, carrots, celery, and garlic. Sauté until softened.
2. Add lentils, diced tomatoes, vegetable broth, oregano, paprika, salt, and pepper.
3. Bring to a boil, then reduce heat and simmer for about 30-45 minutes, or until lentils are tender. Stir in red wine vinegar and adjust seasoning as needed.
4. Serve hot, garnished with chopped parsley.

SERVINGS: 4   PREPPING TIME: 15 MIN   COOKING TIME: 1 HOUR

LOUVANA

INGREDIENTS

2 cups yellow split peas, rinsed
1 large onion, finely chopped
2 carrots, diced
2 stalks celery, diced
3 cloves garlic, minced
6 cups vegetable broth or water
1/4 cup olive oil
1 teaspoon dried thyme
Salt and pepper to taste
Lemon wedges for serving

DIRECTIONS

1. In a large pot, heat olive oil over medium heat. Add onions, carrots, celery, and garlic, and sauté until softened.
2. Add yellow split peas, vegetable broth, thyme, salt, and pepper.
3. Bring to a boil, then reduce heat and simmer for about 1 hour, or until the split peas are soft and the soup has thickened.
4. Optionally, use an immersion blender to partially blend the soup for a creamier texture. Adjust seasoning as needed. Serve hot, with a squeeze of lemon.

Nutritional Information (approximation per serving)*: Calories: 220, Protein: 12g, Carbohydrates: 30g, Fat: 7g, Fiber: 12g, Cholesterol: 0mg, Sodium: 300mg, Potassium: 700mg.
Nutritional Information (approximation per serving)*: Calories: 260, Protein: 15g, Carbohydrates: 40g, Fat: 7g, Fiber: 15g, Cholesterol: 0mg, Sodium: 300mg, Potassium: 700mg.

SERVINGS: 6　　PREPPING TIME: 20 MIN　　COOKING TIME: 40 MIN

PSAROSOUPA

INGREDIENTS

1 kg mixed fish (like snapper, sea bream), cleaned and cut into pieces
1 large onion, chopped
2 carrots, sliced
2 potatoes, diced
2 stalks celery, sliced
1 can (400g) diced tomatoes
6 cups fish or vegetable broth
1/4 cup olive oil
1 lemon, juice and zest
2 bay leaves
Salt and pepper to taste
Fresh parsley, chopped for garnish

DIRECTIONS

1. In a large pot, heat olive oil over medium heat. Add onions, carrots, celery, and potatoes, and sauté for about 5 minutes.
2. Pour in the broth and bring to a boil. Add bay leaves and diced tomatoes.
3. Reduce heat, add fish pieces, and simmer for about 25-30 minutes, or until the fish is cooked through. Add lemon juice and zest, and season with salt and pepper.
4. Serve hot, garnished with chopped parsley.

SERVINGS: 6　　PREPPING TIME: 10 MIN (PLUS OVERNIGHT SOAKING)　　COOKING TIME: 90 MIN

REVITHIA

INGREDIENTS

2 cups dried chickpeas, soaked overnight and drained
1 large onion, chopped
2 cloves garlic, minced
1/4 cup olive oil
1 teaspoon dried rosemary
1 bay leaf
6 cups water
Salt and pepper to taste
Lemon wedges for serving

DIRECTIONS

1. In a large pot, heat olive oil over medium heat. Sauté onion and garlic until translucent.
2. Add soaked and drained chickpeas, water, rosemary, bay leaf, salt, and pepper.
3. Bring to a boil, then reduce heat and simmer, partially covered, for about 1.5 hours or until chickpeas are tender.
4. Remove the bay leaf. Optionally, you can blend a small portion of the soup and add it back to thicken it. Adjust seasoning as needed. Serve hot, with a squeeze of lemon.

Nutritional Information (approximation per serving)*: Calories: 350, Protein: 40g, Carbohydrates: 20g, Fat: 15g, Fiber: 3g, Cholesterol: 60mg, Sodium: 500mg, Potassium: 1000mg.
Nutritional Information (approximation per serving)*: Calories: 290, Protein: 12g, Carbohydrates: 40g, Fat: 10g, Fiber: 11g, Cholesterol: 0mg, Sodium: 200mg, Potassium: 600mg.

SWEETS AND DESSERTS
Ikarian Delights and Sweet Traditions

In Ikaria, sweets and desserts are not just about indulgence; they're a reflection of the island's rich history, local ingredients, and the joy of sharing. This chapter takes you through a delightful journey of Ikarian confectionery, where each recipe tells a story of tradition, celebration, and the sweet side of life.

The Essence of Ikarian Sweets
Ikarian desserts are characterized by their simplicity and the use of fresh, locally sourced ingredients. "Amygdalota" (Greek Almond Cookies) is a prime example, where the delicate flavor of almonds shines through in every bite. These sweets are often enjoyed with a cup of Greek coffee, symbolizing hospitality and warmth.

Baklava: A Layered Delight
Baklava, a sweet that needs no introduction, holds a special place in Ikarian festivities. This layered pastry, with its crunchy nuts and sweet syrup, is a labor of love and a testament to the island's culinary expertise.

Galaktoboureko: Creamy and Dreamy
Galaktoboureko, a creamy custard pie wrapped in golden phyllo, is a dessert that perfectly balances the richness of cream with the crispiness of pastry. It's a dessert that's as indulgent as it is comforting.

Healthier Sweet Options
Reflecting the island's ethos of health and longevity, many Ikarian desserts, like the "Moustalevria" (Grape Must Pudding), incorporate natural sweeteners and nutritious ingredients. These desserts offer a guilt-free way to indulge while still enjoying the benefits of wholesome ingredients.

Festive and Everyday Sweets
From the everyday enjoyment of "Karithopita" (Greek Walnut Cake) to the festive preparations of "Kourabiedes" (Greek Butter Cookies) during holidays, Ikarian sweets and desserts are integral to both daily life and special occasions, marking moments of joy and celebration.

A Sweet End to Meals
In Ikaria, desserts are not just an afterthought but an essential part of the dining experience. They are often shared among friends and family, concluding meals with sweetness and joy.

Cooking Tips and Techniques
Precision in measurements is crucial for the perfect balance of flavors in these sweet treats.
Syrup-soaked desserts like baklava and karithopita are best prepared in advance to allow the syrup to infuse.
When making pastries like galaktoboureko, handle phyllo dough carefully to maintain its delicate texture.

Health and Nutrition Information
While indulgent, these sweets are often enjoyed in moderation as part of the Ikarian diet. Many recipes incorporate nuts, natural sweeteners like honey, and spices, providing a range of health benefits. These desserts are a testament to the balanced approach of Mediterranean eating, where pleasure and health coexist harmoniously.

In conclusion
This chapter is a tribute to the sweet side of Ikaria, where traditional recipes are passed down through generations, and new ones are embraced with the same enthusiasm. These desserts are a testament to the island's rich culinary heritage and the joyous spirit of its people.

RECIPES

- **Amygdalota:** Delicate almond cookies, a perfect blend of sweet and nutty flavors.
- **Baklava:** A classic Greek dessert, featuring layers of phyllo pastry, filled with nuts and soaked in honey syrup.
- **Galaktoboureko:** A custard-filled pastry, that combines creamy texture with the crispiness of phyllo.
- **Halvas me Simigdali:** A semolina and honey halva, enriched with nuts and cinnamon.
- **Karithopita:** A moist and flavorful walnut cake, infused with spices and drenched in syrup.
- **Karydia me Syko:** An elegant dish of walnuts and figs, showcasing the natural sweetness of dried fruits.
- **Kourabiedes:** Traditional Greek butter cookies, dusted with powdered sugar.
- **Loukoumades:** Greek honey puffs, light and golden, drizzled with honey and cinnamon.
- **Moustalevria:** A grape must pudding, a unique and delightful dessert.
- **Sykomaïda:** A fig and walnut cake, embodying the flavors of the Mediterranean.
- **Pasteli:** Greek sesame and honey bars, a crunchy and sweet snack.
- **Paximadia:** Aniseed biscuits, combining the aromatic flavors of anise with a crunchy texture.
- **Portokalopita:** An olive oil and orange cake, moist and fragrant.
- **Sokolatenia** Troufakia: Coffee chocolate truffles, a luxurious treat for chocolate lovers.

SERVINGS: 24 COOKIES   PREPPING TIME: 20 MIN   COOKING TIME: 15 MIN

AMYGDALOTA

INGREDIENTS

3 cups almond flour
1 cup granulated sugar
2 egg whites
1 teaspoon almond extract
1/4 teaspoon salt
Powdered sugar for dusting

DIRECTIONS

1. Preheat oven to 180°C (350°F). Line a baking sheet with parchment paper.
2. In a bowl, mix almond flour, granulated sugar, and salt. In another bowl, beat egg whites until stiff peaks form. Gently fold in the almond extract.
3. Gradually fold the egg whites into the almond flour mixture until well combined.
4. Shape the dough into small balls and place them on the prepared baking sheet.
5. Bake for 15 minutes or until lightly golden.
6. Let cool and dust with powdered sugar before serving.

SERVINGS: 10   PREPPING TIME: 10 MIN   COOKING TIME: 30 MIN

HALVAS ME SIMIGDALI

INGREDIENTS

2 cups semolina
1 cup honey
4 cups water
1/2 cup chopped nuts (walnuts, almonds)
1 teaspoon cinnamon
1/2 cup olive oil

DIRECTIONS

1. In a saucepan, bring water and honey to a boil, then simmer for 5 minutes.
2. In another pan, heat olive oil and add semolina. Stir continuously until golden brown.
3. Slowly pour the honey water into the semolina, stirring constantly to avoid lumps.
4. Add cinnamon and nuts, mix well.
5. Pour the mixture into a greased baking dish and let it cool until set.
6. Cut into pieces and serve.

Nutritional Information (approximation per serving)*: Calories: 120, Protein: 3g, Carbohydrates: 10g, Fat: 8g, Fiber: 2g, Cholesterol: 0mg, Sodium: 25mg, Potassium: 40mg.
Nutritional Information (approximation per serving)*: Calories: 340, Protein: 5g, Carbohydrates: 50g, Fat: 14g, Fiber: 3g, Cholesterol: 0mg, Sodium: 10mg, Potassium: 90mg.

SERVINGS: 24　　　PREPPING TIME: 30 MIN　　　COOKING TIME: 50 MIN

BAKLAVA

INGREDIENTS

1 package phyllo dough, thawed
2 cups chopped nuts (walnuts, pistachios, or almonds)
1 cup butter, melted
1 teaspoon ground cinnamon

<u>Syrup</u>:

1 cup granulated sugar
1 cup water
1/2 cup honey
2 tablespoons lemon juice
1 cinnamon stick

DIRECTIONS

1. Preheat oven to 175°C (350°F). Grease a 9x13-inch baking dish.
2. Mix nuts with ground cinnamon. Set aside.
3. Place a sheet of phyllo in the dish and brush with melted butter. Repeat with half of the phyllo sheets, brushing each with butter.
4. Spread the nut mixture over the layered phyllo.
5. Layer the remaining phyllo sheets on top, brushing each with butter.
6. Cut into diamond or square shapes.
7. Bake for 50 minutes or until golden and crisp.

<u>For the syrup:</u>

1. While baklava is baking, combine sugar, water, honey, lemon juice, and cinnamon sticks in a saucepan.
2. Bring to a boil, then lower the heat and simmer for about 10 minutes.
3. Remove the cinnamon stick.

<u>Final Step:</u>

1. Pour the hot syrup over the cooled baklava.
2. Let it soak for several hours before serving.

Nutritional Information (approximation per serving)*: Calories: 220, Protein: 3g, Carbohydrates: 25g, Fat: 12g, Fiber: 1g, Cholesterol: 15mg, Sodium: 100mg, Potassium: 60mg.

SERVINGS: 12   PREPPING TIME: 30 MIN   COOKING TIME: 45 MIN

GALAKTOBOUREKO

INGREDIENTS

1 package phyllo dough, thawed
1/2 cup butter, melted
4 cups milk
1 cup sugar
1/2 cup semolina
4 eggs
1 teaspoon vanilla extract
Zest of 1 lemon

<u>Syrup</u>:

1 cup sugar
1 cup water
1/2 cup honey
1 cinnamon stick
1 strip of lemon peel

DIRECTIONS

1. Preheat oven to 180°C (350°F). Grease a 9x13-inch baking dish.
2. In a saucepan, heat milk over medium heat. Add sugar and semolina, whisking continuously until thickened.
3. Beat eggs in a bowl. Gradually add some of the hot milk mixture to temper the eggs, then pour the egg mixture back into the saucepan. Stir in vanilla extract and lemon zest. Cook until the mixture is thick.
4. Lay out the phyllo sheets, brushing each with melted butter. Place half of the phyllo sheets in the baking dish.
5. Pour the custard over the phyllo, then cover with the remaining phyllo sheets, again brushing each with butter.
6. Bake for 45 minutes or until golden brown.

<u>For the syrup</u>:

1. In a saucepan, combine sugar, water, honey, cinnamon stick, and lemon peel. Bring to a boil and simmer for 10 minutes.
2. Remove the cinnamon stick and lemon peel.

<u>Final Step</u>:

1. Pour the hot syrup over the hot Galaktoboureko.
2. Allow to cool before cutting into squares to serve.

Nutritional Information (approximation per serving)*: Calories: 390, Protein: 7g, Carbohydrates: 55g, Fat: 16g, Fiber: 1g, Cholesterol: 95mg, Sodium: 180mg, Potassium: 150mg.

SERVINGS: 12   PREPPING TIME: 20 MIN   COOKING TIME: 40 MIN

KARITHOPITA

INGREDIENTS

2 cups finely chopped walnuts
1 cup all-purpose flour
1 teaspoon baking powder
1 teaspoon ground cinnamon
1/2 teaspoon ground cloves
4 eggs, separated
1 cup sugar
1/2 cup olive oil
1/2 cup fresh orange juice
Zest of 1 orange

Syrup:

1 cup sugar
1 cup water
1/2 cup honey
1 cinnamon stick
1 strip of orange peel

DIRECTIONS

1. Preheat oven to 180°C (350°F). Grease and flour a 9x13-inch baking pan.
2. Mix walnuts, flour, baking powder, cinnamon, and cloves.
3. Beat egg whites to stiff peaks.
4. In another bowl, beat egg yolks with sugar until creamy. Mix in olive oil, orange juice, and orange zest.
5. Fold in the walnut mixture, then gently fold in the egg whites.
6. Pour batter into the prepared pan and bake for 40 minutes or until a toothpick inserted comes out clean.

For Syrup:

1. Boil sugar, water, honey, cinnamon, and orange peel for 10 minutes. Remove cinnamon and peel.
2. Pour hot syrup over the hot Karithopita.
3. Cool before serving.

Nutritional Information (approximation per serving)*: Calories: 380, Protein: 6g, Carbohydrates: 50g, Fat: 20g, Fiber: 2g, Cholesterol: 70mg, Sodium: 60mg, Potassium: 150mg.

SERVINGS: 6   PREPPING TIME: 15 MIN   COOKING TIME: 0 MIN

KARYDIA ME SYKO

INGREDIENTS

1 cup dried figs, halved
1 cup walnuts, roughly chopped
1/4 cup honey
1/2 teaspoon ground cinnamon
Zest of 1 orange
A pinch of ground cloves

DIRECTIONS

1. In a bowl, combine the halved figs and chopped walnuts.
2. Drizzle honey over the mixture and sprinkle with ground cinnamon, orange zest, and a pinch of cloves.
3. Gently toss to coat everything evenly. Serve as a dessert or a sweet snack.

SERVINGS: 24 COOKIES   PREPPING TIME: 20 MIN   COOKING TIME: 15 MIN

KOURABIEDES

INGREDIENTS

1 cup unsalted butter, softened
1/2 cup powdered sugar, plus more for coating
1 teaspoon vanilla extract
1 tablespoon brandy
2 cups all-purpose flour
1 cup almonds, finely chopped
A pinch of salt

DIRECTIONS

1. Preheat the oven to 180°C (350°F). Line a baking sheet with parchment paper.
2. In a large bowl, cream together the butter and 1/2 cup powdered sugar until light and fluffy.
3. Stir in vanilla extract and brandy.
4. Gradually mix in flour, almonds, and a pinch of salt until the dough comes together.
5. Shape the dough into small crescents and place them on the prepared baking sheet.
6. Bake for 15 minutes or until lightly golden.
7. Let the cookies cool slightly, then roll them in additional powdered sugar until well-coated.
8. Cool completely on wire racks.

Nutritional Information (approximation per serving)*: Calories: 250, Protein: 4g, Carbohydrates: 35g, Fat: 12g, Fiber: 5g, Cholesterol: 0mg, Sodium: 5mg, Potassium: 300mg.
Nutritional Information (approximation per serving)*: Calories: 180, Protein: 2g, Carbohydrates: 15g, Fat: 12g, Fiber: 1g, Cholesterol: 20mg, Sodium: 5mg, Potassium: 50mg.

SERVINGS: 6 — PREPPING TIME: 15 MIN (PLUS RESTING) — COOKING TIME: 20 MIN

LOUKOUMADES

INGREDIENTS

2 cups all-purpose flour
2 teaspoons active dry yeast
1 teaspoon sugar
1/2 teaspoon salt
1 1/2 cups warm water
Vegetable oil for frying

For the syrup:

1 cup honey
1/2 cup water
1 tablespoon cinnamon
1 teaspoon lemon juice

DIRECTIONS

1. In a bowl, combine flour, yeast, sugar, and salt.
2. Add warm water and mix until a smooth batter forms. Let the batter rest for 1 hour until it rises.
3. Heat oil in a deep fryer or large saucepan to 180°C (350°F).
4. Drop spoonfuls of batter into the hot oil and fry until golden brown.
5. Remove with a slotted spoon and drain on paper towels.

For the syrup:

1. In a saucepan, combine honey, water, cinnamon, and lemon juice. Bring to a boil, then reduce heat and simmer for 5 minutes.
2. Drizzle the hot syrup over the hot loukoumades.

Nutritional Information (approximation per serving)*: Calories: 380, Protein: 6g, Carbohydrates: 50g, Fat: 20g, Fiber: 2g, Cholesterol: 70mg, Sodium: 60mg, Potassium: 150mg.

SERVINGS: 6　　　PREPPING TIME: 10 MIN　　　COOKING TIME: 30 MIN

MOUSTALEVRIA

INGREDIENTS

4 cups grape must (fresh grape juice)
1 cup water
1/2 cup cornflour
1/2 cup sugar (optional)
Cinnamon, crushed walnuts for garnish

DIRECTIONS

1. Mix cornflour with water until smooth. Add grape must, sugar.
2. Cook over medium heat, stirring, until thickens (30 minutes).
3. Pour into dish or bowls, cool, refrigerate.
4. Sprinkle with cinnamon, walnuts before serving.

SERVINGS: 10　　　PREPPING TIME: 20 MIN　　　COOKING TIME: 30 MIN

SYKOMAÏDA

INGREDIENTS

2 cups dried figs, chopped
1 cup walnuts, chopped
1/2 cup sesame seeds
1/2 cup honey
1/4 cup brandy or grape must
1 teaspoon ground cinnamon
1/2 teaspoon ground cloves
Grated zest of 1 orange
Olive oil for greasing

DIRECTIONS

1. Preheat the oven to 180°C (350°F). Grease a baking dish with olive oil.
2. In a large mixing bowl, combine chopped figs, walnuts, sesame seeds, honey, brandy or grape must, cinnamon, cloves, and orange zest.
3. Mix well until all ingredients are evenly distributed.
4. Press the mixture firmly into the prepared baking dish.
5. Bake in the preheated oven for about 30 minutes, or until the top is golden brown.
6. Allow to cool in the dish, then cut into squares or bars.

Nutritional Information (approximation per serving)*: Calories: 180, Protein: 1g, Carbohydrates: 40g, Fat: 1g, Fiber: 1g, Cholesterol: 0mg, Sodium: 10mg, Potassium: 100mg.
Nutritional Information (approximation per serving)*: Calories: 250, Protein: 3g, Carbohydrates: 35g, Fat: 12g, Fiber: 4g, Cholesterol: 0mg, Sodium: 10mg, Potassium: 200mg.

SERVINGS: 12 BARS   PREPPING TIME: 10 MIN   COOKING TIME: 15 MIN

PASTELI

INGREDIENTS

1 cup sesame seeds
1/2 cup honey
1/4 cup sugar
1/4 cup water
Zest of 1 lemon
Zest of 1 orange

DIRECTIONS

1. In a dry skillet, toast the sesame seeds over medium heat until they turn golden brown. Remove them from the skillet and set them aside.
2. In a saucepan, combine the honey, sugar, water, lemon zest, and orange zest.
3. Cook the mixture over medium heat, stirring constantly, until it reaches the soft ball stage (about 250°F or 121°C on a candy thermometer). This should take about 10-15 minutes. Remove the saucepan from heat and quickly stir in the toasted sesame seeds.
4. Pour the mixture into a greased or parchment-lined square pan.
5. While the mixture is still warm, cut it into bars or squares.
6. Allow it to cool and set before serving.

SERVINGS: 20 BISCUITS   PREPPING TIME: 15 MIN   COOKING TIME: 40 MIN

PAXIMADIA

INGREDIENTS

3 cups all-purpose flour
1 cup sugar
3/4 cup olive oil
2 eggs
1 tablespoon aniseed
1 teaspoon baking powder
1/2 teaspoon salt

DIRECTIONS

1. Preheat oven to 350°F (175°C).
2. In a bowl, mix flour, baking powder, aniseed, and salt.
3. In another bowl, beat eggs, sugar, and olive oil.
4. Combine the dry and wet ingredients to form a dough.
5. Shape the dough into a log and place on a baking sheet.
6. Bake for 25 minutes, then remove and slice into 1/2-inch thick biscuits.
7. Place the biscuits back on the baking sheet and bake for another 15 minutes until golden. Let cool before serving.

Nutritional Information (approximation per serving)*: Calories: 150 (per bar), Protein: 2g, Carbohydrates: 23g, Fat: 7g, Fiber: 1g, Cholesterol: 0mg, Sodium: 0mg, Potassium: 70mg.
Nutritional Information (approximation per serving)*: Calories: 220, Protein: 3g, Carbohydrates: 30g, Fat: 10g, Fiber: 1g, Cholesterol: 20mg, Sodium: 60mg, Potassium: 40mg.

SERVINGS: 8   PREPPING TIME: 15 MIN   COOKING TIME: 50 MIN

PORTOKALOPITA

INGREDIENTS

2 cups all-purpose flour
1/2 cup olive oil
3/4 cup sugar
Juice and zest of 2 oranges
3 eggs
1 baking powder
1/2 salt

DIRECTIONS

1. Preheat oven to 350°F (175°C). Grease a 9-inch cake pan. In a bowl, combine flour, baking powder, and salt.
2. In another bowl, beat together eggs, sugar, olive oil, orange zest, and juice until well blended.
3. Gradually mix the dry ingredients into the wet mixture until smooth.
4. Pour the batter into the prepared pan and bake for about 50 minutes, until a toothpick inserted into the center comes out clean. Allow to cool before serving.

SERVINGS: 20 TRUFFLES   PREPPING TIME: 30 MIN   COOKING TIME: 10 MIN

SOKOLATENIA TROUFAKIA

INGREDIENTS

8 oz (225g) dark chocolate, finely chopped
1/2 cup heavy cream
2 tablespoons Greek coffee, finely ground
1 tablespoon granulated sugar
Cocoa powder or crushed nuts for coating
A pinch of sea salt

DIRECTIONS

1. In a small saucepan, heat the heavy cream with the Greek coffee and sugar until it just begins to simmer. Remove from heat and let it steep for 10 minutes.
2. Strain the coffee cream mixture through a fine sieve to remove the grounds, then reheat the cream until it simmers.
3. Place the chopped chocolate in a bowl. Pour the hot coffee-infused cream over the chocolate. Let it sit for a minute and then stir until the chocolate is completely melted and the mixture is smooth. Add a pinch of sea salt and mix well.
4. Allow the mixture to cool, then refrigerate for at least 2 hours or until firm. Once chilled, use a spoon or melon baller to scoop out balls of the chocolate mixture.
5. Roll them quickly with your hands to form truffles. Roll each truffle in cocoa powder or crushed nuts to coat. Store the truffles in the refrigerator in an airtight container.

Nutritional Information (approximation per serving)*: Calories: 320, Protein: 5g, Carbohydrates: 45g, Fat: 14g, Fiber: 1g, Cholesterol: 70mg, Sodium: 180mg, Potassium: 60mg.
Nutritional Information (approximation per serving)*:Calories: 100, Protein: 1g, Carbohydrates: 10g, Fat: 7g, Fiber: 2g, Cholesterol: 5mg, Sodium: 10mg, Potassium: 50mg.

VEGETABLE AND SALAD DISHES
The Heart of Ikarian Cuisine

In Ikaria, vegetables and salads are the cornerstone of every meal, reflecting the island's commitment to health, longevity, and simplicity. This chapter explores the vibrant and varied vegetable dishes that form the backbone of Ikarian cuisine, highlighting the island's lush produce and the creativity of its cooks.

A Celebration of Fresh Produce
Ikarian vegetable dishes are a celebration of the island's fertile land and bountiful gardens. Dishes like "Chorta Vrasta" (Boiled Greens) showcase the natural flavors of fresh, local greens, lightly seasoned and dressed to enhance their inherent goodness.

The Art of Stuffing and Simmering
Ikarian cuisine excels in transforming simple ingredients into extraordinary dishes. "Gemista" (Stuffed Tomatoes and Peppers) is a perfect example, where vegetables are stuffed with flavorful rice and herbs, and then baked to perfection. It's a dish that represents the island's love for stuffed and simmered foods.

Healthy and Nourishing Choices
Ikarians' diet is closely linked to their renowned longevity, and their vegetable dishes are a testament to this. "Fasolakia" (Greek Green Beans) is a typical dish that combines taste with nutrition, simmered in a rich tomato sauce.

Salads: A Daily Staple
In Ikarian households, salads like "Horiatiki" (Greek Village Salad) are a daily staple, providing a refreshing and nutritious complement to meals. Packed with fresh tomatoes, cucumbers, onions, and olives, and topped with feta cheese, these salads are a burst of flavors and health benefits.

Versatility of Vegetables
Ikarian vegetable recipes are versatile and adaptable. "Kolokithokeftedes" (Zucchini Fritters) and "Melitzanes Imam" (Baked Eggplant with Tomato Sauce) demonstrate how vegetables can be transformed into various forms, from fritters to baked dishes, each offering a unique taste experience.

Simplicity and Flavor
The key to Ikarian vegetable dishes lies in their simplicity and the emphasis on natural flavors. "Lemon Roasted Potatoes" is a dish that combines basic ingredients with robust flavors, perfectly embodying the Ikarian approach to cooking.

Cooking Tips and Techniques
For the freshest flavors, use seasonal vegetables and herbs.
When preparing dishes like Dolmadakia and Gemista, patience and care are key to perfectly wrapping and stuffing.
Roasting and stewing are common techniques in these recipes, bringing out the natural sweetness and flavors of the vegetables.

Health and Nutrition Information
This chapter emphasizes the health benefits of a plant-based diet, rich in vitamins, minerals, and antioxidants. The dishes are heart-healthy, often featuring olive oil and a variety of greens and legumes, aligning with both the Mediterranean diet and the principles of the Blue Zones. These recipes offer a delicious way to enjoy vegetables, making them a central part of every meal.

In conclusion

This chapter is not just a collection of recipes; it's a window into the soul of Ikarian cuisine, where vegetables are not just side dishes but stars in their own right. These recipes embody the essence of the Mediterranean diet and offer a taste of Ikaria's culinary heritage and its enduring commitment to health and well-being.

RECIPES

- **Chorta Vrasta:** Simple yet nourishing boiled greens, drizzled with olive oil and lemon.
- **Briam:** A roasted vegetable dish, often referred to as Ikarian ratatouille.
- **Dolmadakia:** Stuffed grape leaves, a perfect blend of rice, herbs, and zesty lemon.
- **Fasolakia:** Ikarian green beans simmered in a tomato-based sauce, a classic comfort dish.
- **Fried Horta:** Crispy fried greens, a delightful combination of texture and flavor.
- **Gemista:** Stuffed tomatoes and peppers, brimming with rice and fresh herbs.
- **Horiatiki Salata:** The quintessential Ikarian village salad, a colorful medley of fresh vegetables.
- **Kolokithia me Avgolemono:** Zucchini in a creamy egg-lemon sauce, a testament to Greek culinary ingenuity.
- **Kolokithokeftedes:** Zucchini fritters, are a delicious way to enjoy this versatile vegetable.
- **Ladera:** A traditional Ikarian vegetable casserole, rich in olive oil and Mediterranean flavors.
- **Lemon Roasted Potatoes:** Crispy and tangy, these potatoes are a staple in Ikarian households.
- **Marathokeftedes:** Fennel fritters, combining the unique taste of fennel with a crunchy exterior.
- **Marathopita:** Fennel pie, a savory pastry that encapsulates the essence of the Mediterranean.
- **Melitzanes Imam:** Baked eggplant with tomato sauce, a dish that balances simplicity with depth of flavor.
- **Patates Yachni:** Ikarian stewed potatoes, a comforting dish with a rich tomato-based sauce.
- **Pligouri Salad:** Bulgur wheat salad, is a refreshing and nutritious choice.
- **Prasorizo:** Ikarian leek and rice, a harmonious blend of subtle flavors.
- **Roka Salata:** Arugula salad, a peppery and fresh dish with a Mediterranean twist.
- **Soufiko:** Ikarian vegetable medley, a vibrant showcase of the island's best produce.
- **Strapatsada:** Ikarian scrambled eggs with tomato, a simple yet flavorful meal.

SERVINGS: 4   PREPPING TIME: 10 MIN   COOKING TIME: 10 MIN

CHORTA VRASTA

INGREDIENTS

1 kg mixed greens (e.g., dandelion, spinach, mustard greens)
1/4 cup olive oil
Juice of 1 lemon
Salt to taste

DIRECTIONS

1. Thoroughly wash the greens to remove any dirt or grit.
2. Bring a large pot of salted water to a boil.
3. Add the greens and boil for about 5-10 minutes or until tender.
4. Drain the greens and press out excess water.
5. Dress with olive oil, lemon juice, and a pinch of salt.
6. Serve warm as a side dish.

SERVINGS: 30 PIECES   PREPPING TIME: 30 MIN   COOKING TIME: 60 MIN

DOLMADAKIA

INGREDIENTS

30 grape leaves, drained and rinsed
1 cup rice, uncooked
1 large onion, finely chopped
1/4 cup olive oil
1/4 cup fresh dill, chopped
1/4 cup fresh mint, chopped
Salt and pepper to taste
Lemon slices for garnish

DIRECTIONS

1. In a pan, sauté onions in olive oil until translucent. Add rice, dill, mint, salt, and pepper, cooking for a few minutes.
2. Lay out a grape leaf, shiny side down. Place a teaspoon of filling near the stem.
3. Fold sides over the filling and roll tightly.
4. Arrange the rolls seam-side down in a pot.
5. Cover with water, add a drizzle of olive oil, and place a plate on top to keep them submerged.
6. Cook over low heat for about 1 hour.
7. Serve warm or cold, garnished with lemon slices.

Nutritional Information (approximation per serving)*: Calories: 150, Protein: 3g, Carbohydrates: 10g, Fat: 12g, Fiber: 4g.
Nutritional Information (approximation per serving)*: Calories: 70, Protein: 1g, Carbohydrates: 10g, Fat 3g, Fiber 1g.

SERVINGS: 4 PREPPING TIME: 10 MIN COOKING TIME: 40 MIN

FASOLAKIA

INGREDIENTS

1 kg green beans, trimmed
1 onion, chopped
2 cloves garlic, minced
1 can diced tomatoes
1/4 cup olive oil
1 teaspoon sugar
Salt and pepper to taste

DIRECTIONS

1. In a large pot, heat olive oil over medium heat. Sauté onions and garlic until softened.
2. Add green beans, tomatoes, sugar, salt, and pepper.
3. Add enough water to half-cover the beans.
4. Bring to a boil, reduce heat, and simmer, covered, for about 40 minutes or until beans are tender. Serve as a side dish.

SERVINGS: 4 PREPPING TIME: 10 MIN COOKING TIME: 5 MIN

FRIED HORTA

INGREDIENTS

1 kg mixed greens (e.g., dandelion greens, spinach)
1/2 cup olive oil for frying
Salt to taste
Lemon wedges for serving

DIRECTIONS

1. Thoroughly wash the greens and pat them dry.
2. Heat olive oil in a large frying pan over medium-high heat.
3. Add the greens in batches and fry until they wilt and become crispy, about 2-3 minutes per side.
4. Remove the greens and drain on paper towels. Sprinkle with salt.
5. Serve hot with lemon wedges on the side.

Nutritional Information (approximation per serving)*: Calories: 180, Protein: 4g, Carbohydrates: 20g, Fat: 10g, Fiber: 6g.
Nutritional Information (approximation per serving)*: Calories: 200, Protein: 3g, Carbohydrates: 10g, Fat: 18g, Fiber: 4g.

SERVINGS: 6   PREPPING TIME: 30 MIN   COOKING TIME: 60 MIN

GEMISTA

INGREDIENTS
6 large tomatoes
6 bell peppers
1 cup rice, uncooked
1 large onion, finely chopped
2 cloves garlic, minced
1/2 cup olive oil
1/2 cup fresh parsley, chopped
1/4 cup fresh mint, chopped
Salt and pepper to taste

DIRECTIONS
1. Preheat the oven to 180°C (350°F).
2. Cut the tops off the tomatoes and peppers. Scoop out the insides of the tomatoes and finely chop them.
3. In a bowl, combine the chopped tomato pulp, rice, onion, garlic, parsley, mint, half of the olive oil, salt, and pepper. Stuff the tomatoes and peppers with this mixture.
4. Place the stuffed vegetables in a baking dish and replace their tops.
5. Drizzle with the remaining olive oil.
6. Bake for about 1 hour, until the vegetables are soft and the rice is cooked. Serve warm.

SERVINGS: 4   PREPPING TIME: 15 MIN   COOKING TIME: 0 MIN

HORIATIKI SALATA

INGREDIENTS
3 tomatoes, cut into wedges
1 cucumber, sliced
1 onion, thinly sliced
1 green bell pepper, sliced
1/2 cup Kalamata olives
200g feta cheese, sliced or crumbled
1/4 cup olive oil
2 tablespoons red wine vinegar
1 teaspoon dried oregano
Salt and pepper to taste

DIRECTIONS
1. In a large bowl, combine tomatoes, cucumber, onion, and bell pepper.
2. Add Kalamata olives and feta cheese on top.
3. Drizzle with olive oil and red wine vinegar.
4. Sprinkle with oregano, salt, and pepper.
5. Toss gently to combine and serve.

Nutritional Information (approximation per serving)*: Calories: 300, Protein: 5g, Carbohydrates: 45g, Fat: 14g, Fiber: 6g.
Nutritional Information (approximation per serving)*: Calories: 250, Protein: 6g, Carbohydrates: 15g, Fat: 20g, Fiber: 4g.

SERVINGS: 4   PREPPING TIME: 15 MIN   COOKING TIME: 20 MIN

KOLOKITHIA ME AVGOLEMONO

INGREDIENTS

4 zucchinis, sliced
1 onion, chopped
2 cups chicken or vegetable broth
2 eggs
Juice of 1 lemon
Salt and pepper to taste
2 tablespoons olive oil

DIRECTIONS

1. In a pot, sauté the onion in olive oil until translucent.
2. Add the zucchini and broth. Bring to a simmer and cook until the zucchini is tender.
3. In a bowl, beat the eggs with the lemon juice.
4. Slowly ladle some of the hot broth into the egg-lemon mixture to temper the eggs.
5. Pour the egg-lemon mixture back into the pot, stirring constantly until the sauce thickens. Do not boil. Season with salt and pepper, and serve.

SERVINGS: 4   PREPPING TIME: 20 MIN   COOKING TIME: 10 MIN

KOLOKITHOKEFTEDES

INGREDIENTS

2 large zucchinis, grated
1 onion, finely chopped
1/2 cup feta cheese, crumbled
1 egg, beaten
2 tablespoons fresh dill, chopped
1/2 cup all-purpose flour
Salt and pepper to taste
Olive oil for frying

DIRECTIONS

1. Place the grated zucchini in a colander, sprinkle with salt, and let sit for 10 minutes. Squeeze out the excess moisture.
2. In a bowl, combine the zucchini, onion, feta, egg, dill, flour, salt, and pepper.
3. Heat olive oil in a frying pan.
4. Drop spoonfuls of the zucchini mixture into the hot oil and flatten slightly.
5. Fry until golden brown on both sides.
6. Drain on paper towels and serve hot.

Nutritional Information (approximation per serving)*: Calories: 150, Protein: 6g, Carbohydrates: 10g, Fat: 10g, Fiber: 3g.

Nutritional Information (approximation per serving)*: Calories: 200, Protein: 6g, Carbohydrates: 15g, Fat: 12g, Fiber: 2g.

SERVINGS: 4　　　PREPPING TIME: 15 MIN　　　COOKING TIME: 45 MIN

LADERA

INGREDIENTS

4 large potatoes, peeled and sliced
2 zucchinis, sliced
1 eggplant, sliced
1 onion, chopped
3 tomatoes, chopped
1/2 cup olive oil
1/2 cup water
2 garlic cloves, minced
1 teaspoon dried oregano
Salt and pepper to taste

DIRECTIONS

1. Preheat the oven to 180°C (350°F).
2. In a large baking dish, layer the potatoes, zucchinis, eggplant, and onion.
3. Sprinkle the garlic, oregano, salt, and pepper over the vegetables.
4. Spread the chopped tomatoes on top.
5. Drizzle the olive oil and water over the vegetables.
6. Cover with foil and bake for 45 minutes or until the vegetables are tender.

SERVINGS: 4　　　PREPPING TIME: 15 MIN　　　COOKING TIME: 0 MIN

LEMON ROASTED POTATOES

INGREDIENTS

1 kg potatoes, peeled and cut into wedges
1/3 cup olive oil
Juice of 2 lemons
2 cloves garlic, minced
1 tablespoon dried oregano
Salt and pepper to taste
Fresh parsley, chopped for garnish

DIRECTIONS

1. Preheat the oven to 200°C (400°F).
2. In a large bowl, mix together olive oil, lemon juice, garlic, oregano, salt, and pepper.
3. Add potato wedges to the bowl and toss to coat evenly.
4. Spread the potatoes in a single layer on a baking sheet.
5. Roast for about 45 minutes, or until golden brown and crispy, turning occasionally.
6. Garnish with fresh parsley before serving.

Nutritional Information (approximation per serving)*: Calories: 250, Protein: 4g, Carbohydrates: 30g, Fat: 14g, Fiber: 6g.
Nutritional Information (approximation per serving)*: Calories: 300, Protein: 5g, Carbohydrates: 40g, Fat: 15g, Fiber: 5g.

SERVINGS: 4   PREPPING TIME: 20 MIN   COOKING TIME: 10 MIN

MARATHOKEFTEDES

INGREDIENTS

2 cups fennel, finely chopped
1 onion, finely chopped
1/2 cup all-purpose flour
1 egg, beaten
2 tablespoons dill, chopped
Salt and pepper to taste
Olive oil for frying

DIRECTIONS

1. In a bowl, combine the fennel, onion, flour, egg, dill, salt, and pepper.
2. Heat olive oil in a frying pan over medium heat.
3. Form the fennel mixture into small patties and fry until golden brown on both sides.
4. Drain on paper towels and serve hot.

SERVINGS: 6   PREPPING TIME: 30 MIN   COOKING TIME: 40 MIN

MARATHOPITA

INGREDIENTS

1 roll phyllo dough
2 cups fennel, finely chopped
1 onion, finely chopped
2 eggs, beaten
1/2 cup feta cheese, crumbled
1/4 cup dill, chopped
Olive oil
Salt and pepper to tasteg

DIRECTIONS

1. Preheat the oven to 180°C (350°F).
2. Sauté the fennel and onion in olive oil until softened.
3. Let cool, then mix in the eggs, feta, dill, salt, and pepper.
4. Lay out a sheet of phyllo dough, brush with olive oil, and place another sheet on top. Repeat with the remaining phyllo.
5. Spread the fennel mixture over the phyllo.
6. Roll up the phyllo around the filling and place in a greased baking dish.
7. Brush the top with olive oil and bake for 40 minutes or until golden brown.

Nutritional Information (approximation per serving)*: Calories: 180, Protein: 5g, Carbohydrates: 15g, Fat: 10g, Fiber: 3g.
Nutritional Information (approximation per serving)*: Calories: 300, Protein: 9g, Carbohydrates: 30g, Fat: 17g, Fiber: 3g.

SERVINGS: 4   PREPPING TIME: 20 MIN   COOKING TIME: 40 MIN

MELITZANES IMAM

INGREDIENTS

4 medium eggplants
1/4 cup olive oil
2 onions, finely chopped
2 cloves garlic, minced
2 tomatoes, chopped
2 tablespoons tomato paste
1/2 cup fresh parsley, chopped
1 teaspoon sugar
Salt and pepper to taste
Feta cheese for garnish (optional)

DIRECTIONS

1. Preheat oven to 180°C (350°F).
2. Cut the eggplants in half lengthwise and scoop out the flesh, leaving a thin shell.
3. Chop the scooped-out flesh.
4. In a pan, heat half of the olive oil. Sauté onions and garlic until translucent.
5. Add the chopped eggplant, tomatoes, tomato paste, parsley, sugar, salt, and pepper. Cook for 10 minutes.
6. Stuff the eggplant shells with the mixture. Place in a baking dish.
7. Drizzle with remaining olive oil. Bake for 30 minutes, or until eggplants are tender.
8. Garnish with feta cheese before serving.

SERVINGS: 4   PREPPING TIME: 10 MIN   COOKING TIME: 40 MIN

PATATES YACHNI

INGREDIENTS

1 kg potatoes, peeled and cut into chunks
1 onion, chopped
2 cloves garlic, minced
1 can diced tomatoes
1/2 cup olive oil
1 teaspoon dried oregano
Salt and pepper to taste
2 cups water

DIRECTIONS

1. In a large pot, heat the olive oil over medium heat. Sauté the onion and garlic until translucent.
2. Add the potatoes, diced tomatoes, oregano, salt, pepper, and water.
3. Bring to a boil, then reduce heat and simmer for about 40 minutes, or until the potatoes are tender and the sauce has thickened.
4. Adjust seasoning and serve.

Nutritional Information (approximation per serving)*: Calories: 220, Protein: 5g, Carbohydrates: 20g, Fat: 14g, Fiber: 7g.
Nutritional Information (approximation per serving)*: Calories: 300, Protein: 6g, Carbohydrates: 45g, Fat: 14g, Fiber: 6g.

SERVINGS: 4   PREPPING TIME: 20 MIN   COOKING TIME: 15 MIN

PLIGOURI SALAD

INGREDIENTS

1 cup bulgur wheat (pligouri)
2 cups water
1 cucumber, diced
2 tomatoes, diced
1/2 red onion, finely chopped
1/4 cup fresh parsley, chopped
1/4 cup fresh mint, chopped
1/4 cup olive oil
Juice of 1 lemon
Salt and pepper to taste
Feta cheese, crumbled (optional)

DIRECTIONS

1. In a pot, bring water to a boil. Add bulgur wheat, reduce heat, and simmer until tender and water is absorbed, about 15 minutes.
2. Let the bulgur cool to room temperature.
3. In a large bowl, combine the cooled bulgur with cucumber, tomatoes, red onion, parsley, and mint.
4. In a small bowl, whisk together olive oil, lemon juice, salt, and pepper.
5. Pour the dressing over the salad and toss to combine.
6. Top with crumbled feta cheese if desired and serve.

SERVINGS: 4   PREPPING TIME: 15 MIN   COOKING TIME: 25 MIN

PRASORIZO

INGREDIENTS

4 leeks, cleaned and sliced
1 cup rice, uncooked
1/4 cup olive oil
2 cloves garlic, minced
2 1/2 cups vegetable broth
Salt and pepper to taste
Lemon wedges for serving

DIRECTIONS

1. In a large skillet, heat the olive oil over medium heat. Add leeks and garlic and sauté until soft.
2. Stir in rice and cook for 2 minutes.
3. Add vegetable broth, salt, and pepper. Bring to a boil.
4. Reduce heat, cover, and simmer for about 20 minutes, until the rice is cooked and liquid is absorbed.
5. Serve with lemon wedges.

Nutritional Information (approximation per serving)*: Calories: 250, Protein: 6g, Carbohydrates: 35g, Fat: 11g, Fiber: 8g.
Nutritional Information (approximation per serving)*: Calories: 300, Protein: 5g, Carbohydrates: 45g, Fat: 12g, Fiber: 3g.

SERVINGS: 4 PREPPING TIME: 10 MIN COOK

ROKA SALAT

INGREDIENTS

4 cups arugula (roka)
1/2 cup cherry tomatoes, halved
1/4 red onion, thinly sliced
1/4 cup Kalamata olives
1/4 cup grated Parmesan cheese
1/4 cup olive oil
2 tablespoons balsamic vinegar
Salt and pepper to taste

DIRECTIONS

1. In a large bowl, combine arugula, cherry tomatoes, red onion, and olives.
2. In a small bowl, whisk together olive oil, balsamic vinegar, salt, and pepper.
3. Pour the dressing over the salad and toss gently.
4. Sprinkle with grated Parmesan cheese before serving.

SERVINGS: 4 PREPPING TIME: 15 MIN COOKING TIME: 30 MIN

SOUFIKO

INGREDIENTS

1 eggplant, sliced
2 zucchinis, sliced
2 bell peppers, sliced
2 tomatoes, sliced
1 onion, sliced
2 cloves garlic, minced
1/4 cup olive oil
Salt and pepper to taste
Fresh herbs (e.g., oregano, parsley), chopped

DIRECTIONS

1. Heat olive oil in a large skillet over medium heat.
2. Sauté onion and garlic until softened.
3. Add eggplant, zucchinis, and bell peppers. Cook until they start to soften.
4. Add tomatoes, salt, and pepper. Cook until all vegetables are tender but still hold their shape.
5. Garnish with fresh herbs and serve either hot or at room temperature.

Nutritional Information (approximation per serving)*: Calories: 200, Protein: 4g, Carbohydrates: 10g, Fat: 16g, Fiber: 2g.

Nutritional Information (approximation per serving)*: Calories: 180, Protein: 3g, Carbohydrates: 20g, Fat: 10g, Fiber: 6g.

PREPPING TIME: 10 MIN   COOKING TIME: 20 MIN

STRAPATSADA

INGREDIENTS

4 large eggs
2 ripe tomatoes, grated
1 onion, finely chopped
2 tablespoons olive oil
Salt and pepper to taste
Feta cheese, crumbled (optional)

DIRECTIONS

1. Heat olive oil in a frying pan. Add the chopped onion and sauté until translucent.
2. Add the grated tomatoes, salt, and pepper. Cook until the mixture thickens.
3. Beat the eggs and add them to the pan, stirring constantly until they are softly scrambled.
4. Optionally, sprinkle with crumbled feta cheese.
5. Serve hot with crusty bread.

SERVINGS: 4   PREPPING TIME: 15 MIN   COOKING TIME: 25 MIN

BRIAM

INGREDIENTS

2 medium zucchinis, sliced
2 medium eggplants, sliced
2 large potatoes, peeled and sliced
2 large tomatoes, sliced
1 large red onion, sliced
2 cloves garlic, minced
1/4 cup extra virgin olive oil
1 teaspoon dried oregano
1 teaspoon dried thyme
Salt and pepper to taste
Fresh parsley for garnish (optional)

DIRECTIONS

1. Preheat your oven to 375°F (190°C).
2. In a large baking dish, layer the sliced zucchinis, eggplants, potatoes, tomatoes, and red onion, alternating the vegetables in an overlapping pattern.
3. Sprinkle minced garlic over the vegetables.
4. Drizzle the olive oil evenly over the vegetables.
5. Season with dried oregano, dried thyme, salt, and pepper.
6. Cover the baking dish with aluminum foil and bake in the preheated oven for 30 minutes.
7. Remove the foil and bake for an additional 15 minutes or until the vegetables are tender and lightly browned.
8. Garnish with fresh parsley if desired before serving.

Nutritional Information (approximation per serving)*: Calories: 200, Protein: 10g, Carbohydrates: 8g, Fat: 14g, Fiber: 2g.

Nutritional Information (approximation per serving)*: Calories: 240, Protein: 4g, Carbohydrates: 25g, Fat: 15g, Fiber: 6g, Cholesterol: 0mg, Sodium: 320mg, Potassium: 800mg.

STORIES SECTION

In the heart of this cookbook, nestled between recipes that capture the essence of Ikarian cuisine, lies a chapter unlike any other. This section weaves a tapestry of personal stories, a collection of narratives offering a glimpse into the lives of those who have shaped the culinary heritage of Ikaria. These aren't merely tales of ingredients and techniques but stories of the people behind the recipes, each carrying the flavor of their experience, tradition, and the island's bountiful nature.

As we journey through this chapter, we delve into the personal histories that inspired the creation of this recipe book. The names have been lovingly altered to honor the privacy of those who shared their lives with me, yet the authenticity and spirit of their stories remain untouched. These narratives serve as a bridge, connecting the reader not only to Ikaria's rich culinary culture but also to the island's very soul, where every meal is a celebration of life and every ingredient tells a story.

Through these pages, I invite you to step into the kitchens and gardens of Ikaria, sit at the tables where families gather, and experience the warmth and hospitality that define this unique corner of the world. These stories are an invitation to understand why a chapter of tales finds its place in a cookbook: because to truly appreciate the dishes of Ikaria, one must first understand the people who craft them, the land that nourishes them, and the traditions that have passed these recipes down through generations.

Welcome to the stories of Ikaria. May they enrich your understanding of the recipes that follow and inspire you to weave some of the island's magic into your culinary creations.

THE OLIVE GROVE OF WISDOM

On a warm summer evening in Ikaria, young Yiannis found himself wandering through his family's olive grove. The trees, gnarled and ancient, seemed to whisper stories of the past. Yiannis sat under his favorite tree, its branches heavy with silvery leaves and olives.

His grandfather, Papou Nikos, joined him, carrying a basket of freshly baked bread and a jar of their homemade olive oil. "This tree," Papou began, pointing to the one they sat under, "was planted by your great-great-grandfather. It has seen many seasons, just like our family."

Yiannis listened intently as Papou recounted the story of how, during a particularly harsh winter, this tree was the only one that bore fruit, saving their family from scarcity. "It taught us resilience," Papou said, his eyes gleaming with pride. "No matter how tough the winter, spring always follows. Just like this tree, we must be steadfast and patient."

They dipped the bread in the oil, its rich flavor a testament to the tree's legacy. "One day, Yiannis, this grove will be yours. Remember, these trees are more than just plants. They are bearers of our family's strength and endurance."

As the sun dipped below the horizon, casting a golden glow over the grove, Yiannis felt a deep connection to his heritage. The olive grove was more than just land; it was a living history of his family's resilience and hope.

A MORNING CATCH, AN OLD FRIEND

The first rays of the Ikarian sun cast a gentle glow over the harbor as Manolis, a seasoned fisherman, returned from his early morning endeavors. His catch was modest but included a splendid sea bream, its scales shimmering in the morning light.

As Manolis tethered his boat, a familiar figure caught his eye—a childhood friend strolling along the shore, someone he hadn't seen in years. Their eyes met, and a moment of recognition sparked a heartfelt reunion. Warm smiles and hearty greetings were exchanged as memories of their shared past rushed back.

In a spontaneous gesture of Ikarian hospitality, Manolis invited his friend for breakfast by the sea. It was an opportune moment to reminisce and share stories that time had gently folded away.

Near his boat, on a small grill, Manolis began preparing the sea bream. He divulged his simple secret for the perfect grill—a marinade of local herbs and a hint of Ikarian wine, a legacy recipe from his family. The dish was a testament to the island's culinary philosophy: fresh ingredients, uncomplicated preparation, and a profound respect for the sea's offerings.

Sitting on a rustic bench by the water, the two friends enjoyed the grilled fish, its aroma blending with the sea breeze. They spoke of life's journey, the roads traveled, and the enduring beauty of their island. The grilled bream was more than a meal—it symbolized a connection to their roots, a celebration of lasting friendship, and the timeless charm of Ikarian life.

The simple breakfast of grilled seabream shared on a tranquil shore captured the soul of Ikaria—not just in the dish's flavors but in the laughter, the tales, and the revival of a bond that had stood the test of time.

DOLMADAKIA: THE HEART OF THE FESTIVAL OF PANAGIA

As the Festival of Panagia unfolds in the warmth of an Ikarian summer, the air buzzes with communal joy, rich with the scents of traditional Ikarian cuisine. In the midst of this vibrant celebration stands Yiayia Maria, the matriarch of a local family, at the heart of a treasured ritual: the making of Dolmadakia.

Surrounded by her eager grandchildren in the family's sunlit kitchen, Yiayia Maria shares the story behind Dolmadakia as she skillfully prepares the dish. Each grape leaf becomes a canvas, the rice filling mixed with herbs and a zest of lemon, a testament to the island's bountiful nature. With experienced hands, she narrates how this dish has been a festival staple, a connector of generations woven deeply into their family history.

With every fold and roll of the grape leaves, Yiayia Maria imparts wisdom. She speaks of the importance of patience, the delicate balance of flavors, and how each family in Ikaria adds their personal touch to the recipe. It's not just the technique that matters, she explains, but the stories and love infused into each bite.

The grandchildren absorb not only the culinary skills but also the stories of past festivals—tales of kinship, laughter shared around heaped plates of Dolmadakia, and ancestors who celebrated just as they do today. In these moments, the dish transcends its ingredients, becoming a vessel for heritage, celebrating life's continuity.

As night descends and the festival reaches its zenith, the family gathers with others in the village. The Dolmadakia, beautifully presented, symbolize unity, the resilience of traditions, and a bridge between past and present.

Under the starlit sky, with music serenading the air, the community comes together, sharing stories, laughter, and food. Yiayia Maria watches, her heart swelling with pride, as her grandchildren savor the Dolmadakia, understanding the profound legacy they carry within each delicate roll.

In this celebration, the Festival of Panagia transcends an event; it becomes a living tapestry of Ikarian culture, where food like Dolmadakia nourishes the body and feeds the soul, weaving stories and memories into the essence of community life.

A BAKER'S SUNRISE:
THE IKARIAN BREAD LEGACY

In the tranquility of the Ikarian dawn, as the first hints of sunlight kiss the Aegean Sea, the village bakery—a modest, age-old edifice—comes to life. Amidst the stone walls steeped in history, Nikos, the venerable baker, begins his day's work. For Nikos, baking is not merely a profession but a cherished ritual, a tie to the island's legacy that he upholds with pride.

As Nikos prepares the dough, he recalls tales passed down from his grandfather, each narrative woven into the fabric of Ikarian life, much like the bread he bakes is a staple on every local table. He speaks of times when flour was scarce and how the islanders innovated with what little they had, creating bread that was humble yet fulfilling.

In the stillness of his bakery, with hands dusted in flour, Nikos shares his philosophy on baking: "Bread is like life," he muses, "simple ingredients coming together to create something sustaining." The dough under his palms—a blend of local wheat, a touch of salt from the sea, and water as clear as the Ikarian skies—is a testament to the island's bountiful nature.

As the dough rises, the baker stokes the wood-fired oven, its flames a dance of warmth and tradition. The oven, an heirloom itself, has baked countless loaves, each with a story of the day it was made. Nikos explains how heat is not merely about temperature but a catalyst that transforms the dough into a golden, crusty loaf, embodying the spirit of Ikaria.

With the village awakening, the aroma of fresh bread meanders through the narrow streets, signaling the new day's beginning. Villagers, young and old, stop by not just for bread but for a moment of connection with Nikos, whose bakery serves as much as a community hub as it is a place of business.

Each loaf that emerges from the oven carries the essence of Ikaria—resilience, community, and a deep-seated respect for the simple joys of life. As families gather to savor the bread, there's a silent acknowledgment of the heritage it represents, a heritage kept alive by the hands of bakers like Nikos.

Nikos's bread is a reminder of the island's enduring traditions, a daily celebration of a community that finds joy in the simplicity of life and in the timeless art of baking bread, a

UNDER THE FIG TREE:
A TASTE OF NOSTALGIA

In the heart of Ikaria stands an ancient fig tree, its branches laden with sweet fruit, a silent witness to generations of laughter and conversations. Beneath its shade, Kostas, an elderly man with eyes twinkling with memories of bygone summers, slices into a moist Fig and Walnut Cake, instantly transported back to his childhood under this very tree with his dearest friend, Yiannis.

Kostas reminisces about those carefree days when time seemed endless, and their only concern was the adventures that lay ahead. The fig tree was their sanctuary, a place of shared secrets, dreams, and, most importantly, the delicious treats they pilfered from their kitchens.

"The best figs are always the ones that seem just out of reach," Kostas chuckles, remembering how they competed to climb higher and claim the ripest fruits. His mother, aware of their escapades, would bake a Fig and Walnut Cake using the figs they gathered— a simple yet rich confection that harmonized the island's bounty: the natural sweetness of figs and the earthy crunch of walnuts.

This cake became more than just a dessert; it symbolized their friendship, encapsulating their shared joys and sorrows. Each summer, the arrival of fig season was eagerly anticipated, heralding the return of their beloved cake.

As the years unfolded, life led them down separate paths, yet the memories of those summers under the fig tree endured. Now, as Kostas sits alone, the cake's sweet aroma evokes images of a youthful Yiannis, his laughter resonating through the air.

Preparing the cake now, Kostas adheres to the same recipe, each step a ritual that reconnects him with those golden days. With every slice, he honors the enduring bond of friendship and the simple pleasures that define life in Ikaria.

Offering a piece to a passing neighbor, Kostas shares not merely a slice of cake but a slice of history—a story of youth, friendship, and the timeless joy found under the fig tree. The cake, much like their friendship, stands as a testament to the island's spirit—wholesome, enduring, and profoundly heartfelt.

LADENIA: THE HEARTBEAT OF IKARIA

Under the golden hue of an Ikarian sunset, the village of Karkinagri comes alive with the aroma of Ladenia, a dish as humble as it is flavorful, reflecting the essence of the island's culinary simplicity. At the center of this bustling scene is Theodora, a baker whose hands have shaped more than just dough throughout her life. Her Ladenia, renowned across the island for its crisp crust and savory topping, is about to become the centerpiece of the village's annual gathering.

Ladenia, often heralded as Ikaria's answer to pizza, stands as a testament to the ingenuity of its people, crafted from ingredients that narrate the land's generosity. Theodora, with a smile as warm as her oven, begins her day at dawn, kneading the dough with an affection that only years of baking could instill. Flour, water, olive oil, and a whisper of yeast transform under her skilled hands into a canvas awaiting adornment.

As the dough rises, Theodora prepares the topping with the same care and attention she devotes to her garden. Tomatoes, ripe and bursting with the taste of the Aegean sun, are sliced thin. Onions, harvested at the peak of their sweetness, are finely chopped. A generous drizzle of olive oil, a scattering of oregano, and a pinch of salt complete the picture.

With the Ladenia assembled and the oven's heat enveloping the dish, Theodora's kitchen becomes a place of magic. The crust bakes to a perfect golden brown, the tomatoes soften into a sweet, tangy layer, and the onions lend a subtle bite, their flavors melding in a harmony as ancient as the island itself.

As evening falls and the villagers gather, Theodora's Ladenia takes its place at the table, amidst stories of the sea and the laughter of children at play. Each bite serves as a reminder of the island's beauty, a blend of simplicity and depth that defines Ikarian cuisine.

For Theodora, Ladenia is more than just a dish; it is a narrative of resilience, a celebration of community, and a symbol of the joy found in life's simple pleasures. Sharing it with the village, she weaves her story into the tapestry of Ikarian tradition, ensuring that with every slice, the legacy of her craft and the spirit of the island continue to thrive.

In the warmth of shared meals and stories, the villagers of Karkinagri find not just nourishment but a sense of belonging. Ladenia, with its humble origins and rich flavors, serves as a reminder that in Ikaria, the greatest joys are those that are shared. In Theodora's hands, this traditional dish becomes an offering of love, a testament to the island's enduring bond with its past and its hopeful gaze toward the future.

THE LOST RECIPE OF YIAYIA: A FAMILY'S CULINARY HERITAGE REDISCOVERED

In a quaint village in Ikaria, nestled among the rolling hills and overlooking the Aegean Sea, there lived a family who had gradually lost touch with their culinary heritage. Yiayia Maria, the matriarch, was once celebrated for her exceptional cooking abilities, particularly her mouthwatering Fasolada, a traditional Ikarian bean soup known for its heartwarming qualities.

Years after her passing, her grandson Giorgos, while rummaging through the old family house, discovered an old, worn notebook. It was Yiayia Maria's recipe book, filled with her handwritten recipes and culinary secrets. Among the pages, he found the recipe for Fasolada, marked by tomato splashes and notes scribbled in the margins.

Overwhelmed with nostalgia, Giorgos resolved to recreate this beloved recipe. He gathered his family, including distant cousins, embarking on a culinary journey guided by Yiayia Maria's meticulous instructions. Together, they soaked the beans, chopped the vegetables, and lovingly simmered the soup, channeling the patience and care that Yiayia Maria once poured into her cooking.

As the soup bubbled away, the kitchen resonated with stories of Yiayia Maria, sparking laughter and tears as they reminisced about her life and the meals shared in her presence. The rich aroma of the Fasolada filled the air, evoking memories long cherished.

When it came time to dine, a hush fell over the table as they tasted the first spoonfuls. The Fasolada was more than a mere dish; it was a piece of their history, a testament to Yiayia Maria's enduring legacy. It drew the family closer, bridging the distance time had imposed.

Rediscovering Yiayia Maria's Fasolada recipe marked a new chapter for the family. They began to meet more frequently, with each gathering centered around a different recipe from Yiayia's cookbook, thereby strengthening their familial ties and honoring her memory through the flavors she had so lovingly bequeathed.

THE SHEPHERD'S MIDDAY MEAL: A LEGACY OF SIMPLICITY AND FLAVOR

In the rugged, sun-drenched hills of Ikaria, there lived an old shepherd named Kostas. Every day, he led his flock across the sprawling landscapes, embracing the solitude and beauty of nature. Kostas was known for his simplicity and a deep love for traditional Ikarian cuisine, particularly his Fakes Soupa (lentil soup), a dish as humble and hearty as his way of life.

One sunny afternoon, as the bells of his sheep echoed in the distance, Kostas set up a small, makeshift kitchen under the shade of an olive tree. He began preparing his midday meal, a ritual he cherished deeply. With a portable stove, a pot, and a few simple ingredients from his satchel—lentils, onions, a splash of olive oil, and a handful of fresh herbs—he started cooking.

As the soup simmered, a group of hikers passed by. Drawn by the inviting aroma, they approached Kostas, who welcomed them with his trademark warm smile. He eagerly shared his Fakes Soupa with them, serving it in rustic bowls accompanied by crusty bread and a few olives.

The hikers were amazed at the depth of flavor Kostas had achieved with such basic ingredients. They sat together, enjoying the meal and exchanging stories. Kostas spoke passionately about Ikarian cuisine, emphasizing the importance of simplicity and the use of fresh, local ingredients. He shared his recipe for Fakes Soupa, a dish passed down from his mother and refined over the years.

As the sun began to set, the hikers bid farewell to Kostas, enriched not just by the hearty meal but also by the wisdom he imparted. They left with a newfound appreciation for the simplicity and authenticity of Ikarian cuisine, inspired by a shepherd's love for his land and its bounty.

HEALTH AND NUTRITION INFORMATION
Ikarian Cuisine: A Fusion of Mediterranean Diet and Blue Zone Wisdom

Ikarian cuisine is a harmonious blend of the Mediterranean diet and the principles of Blue Zone diets, both of which contribute significantly to longevity and wellness. The island of Ikaria is not only a part of the Mediterranean but also recognized as one of the world's Blue Zones, regions where people live exceptionally long and healthy lives.

Core Elements of Ikarian Diet:

- <u>Olive Oil</u>: Integral to both Mediterranean and Blue Zone diets, olive oil is a healthy fat source, rich in monounsaturated fats and antioxidants, aiding in heart health and longevity.
- <u>Legumes</u>: Central to Ikarian meals, legumes like lentils, chickpeas, and beans are potent sources of plant-based protein, fiber, and essential nutrients, supporting a balanced diet and long life.
- <u>Leafy Greens and Vegetables</u>: Abundant consumption of greens and vegetables, rich in vitamins, minerals, and dietary fiber, aligns with both the Mediterranean and Blue Zone dietary guidelines for optimal health.
- <u>Fish and Seafood</u>: Regular inclusion of fish provides omega-3 fatty acids, beneficial for cardiovascular and brain health, a common feature in both diets.
- <u>Moderate Meat and Dairy Intake</u>: Echoing Blue Zone principles, meat is consumed sparingly, focusing on quality over quantity. Dairy, primarily cheese and yogurt, is consumed in moderation.
- <u>Herbs and Spices</u>: The use of herbs not only adds flavor but also provides anti-inflammatory and antimicrobial benefits, essential in both diet types.

Enhanced Longevity: Ikaria, as a Blue Zone, demonstrates the significant impact of diet on lifespan. A balanced, natural diet is key to the islanders' remarkable longevity.

Disease Prevention: Both diets contribute to a reduced risk of chronic diseases such as heart disease, diabetes, and certain cancers.

Mental Clarity and Health: The nutrient-rich diet supports brain health, reducing the risks of cognitive decline and mental health issues.

Adopting the Ikarian Diet within the Blue Zone:

- Embrace more plant-centric meals, a key aspect of the Blue Zones.
- Opt for natural, unprocessed foods as a staple.
- Include healthy fats like olive oil, nuts, and seeds.
- Engage in communal eating, valuing social connections as part of mealtime.
- Balance physical activity with dietary habits, as per Blue Zone lifestyles.

Incorporating elements of the Ikarian diet into daily life means embracing a lifestyle that goes beyond nutrition.
It's about community, simplicity, and finding joy in everyday living, principles that are central to both the Mediterranean and Blue Zone ways of life.

COOKING TIPS AND TECHNIQUES

In this section, we delve into the practical aspects of Ikarian cooking, sharing tips and techniques that will help you master the art of preparing these healthful and delicious meals. Whether you're a novice or an experienced cook, these insights will enhance your culinary skills and bring the authentic flavors of Ikaria to your kitchen.

1. Embracing Simplicity in Cooking

Ikarian cuisine is about simplicity and making the most of fresh, local ingredients. Focus on the quality of ingredients rather than complex cooking methods.
Use fresh herbs to add depth and flavor without overpowering the natural taste of primary ingredients.

2. The Art of Slow Cooking

Many traditional Ikarian dishes, like stews and legumes, benefit from slow cooking. This method allows flavors to meld and deepen, resulting in rich and satisfying dishes.
Experiment with low and slow cooking methods, either in a traditional oven or with modern slow cookers.

3. Perfecting Seafood Dishes

Freshness is key for seafood. If you have access to fresh, local seafood, use it the same day for the best flavor.
For grilling fish, ensure your grill is hot and well-oiled to prevent sticking. Simplicity is key – a bit of olive oil, lemon, and herbs are often all you need.

4. Mastering Phyllo Dough

Working with phyllo can be intimidating, but patience is crucial. Keep the dough covered with a damp cloth to prevent drying out.
Brush each layer lightly with olive oil or melted butter for flakiness and flavor.

5. Utilizing Olive Oil

Olive oil is a staple in Ikarian cooking. Use high-quality extra virgin olive oil for dressings and low-heat cooking to preserve its flavor and health benefits.
For sautéing or frying, regular olive oil is more suitable due to its higher smoke point.

6. Balancing Flavors

Ikarian cuisine is about balancing flavors – the tanginess of lemon, the earthiness of olive oil, and the freshness of herbs.

Taste as you go and adjust seasonings to find the right balance for your palate.

7. Incorporating Legumes and Grains

Soak beans and legumes overnight to reduce cooking time and enhance digestibility.

When cooking grains like bulgur or rice, ensure an adequate water-to-grain ratio for the perfect texture.

8. Vegetable Preparation

Embrace the variety of vegetables in Ikarian cuisine. Learn to cut them in ways that maximize their texture and flavor in dishes.

Roasting vegetables is a simple way to enhance their natural sweetness.

9. Making Homemade Breads and Pastries

Kneading dough thoroughly is key to developing gluten, which gives bread its texture.

For pastries, keep all ingredients, including butter and water, cold for a flaky result.

Bread and pastry doughs benefit from patient and thorough kneading to develop texture and flavor.

Utilizing local ingredients like fresh herbs, cheeses, and olive oil enhances the authenticity and taste of each recipe.

10. Preserving and Canning

Ikarian cuisine makes use of preserved foods, such as sun-dried tomatoes or pickled vegetables.

Learn basic canning techniques to enjoy seasonal produce year-round.

APPETIZERS AND DIPS

Aginares a la Polita..4
Chickpea Fritters..5
Fava..5
Kaparosalata...6
Melitzanosalata..6
Pantzaria..7
Riganada..7
Saganaki...8
Skordostoumbi..8
Skordalia..9
Tzatziki...9

BREADS AND PASTRIES

Boureki...12
Eliopsomo..12
Choriatiko Psomi..13
Flaounes...14
Kleftiko Pita..15
Kreatopita..16
Kotopita Icaria..17
Kremmydopita..18
Ladenia..19
Myzithropitakia..19
Pitarakia..20
Prasopita...20
Psomi me Elies...21
Sfouggato..22
Tsoureki..23

MEAT AND POULTRY DISHES

Giaourtlou..26
Lachanodolmades..26

Gyros..27
Keftedes..28
Kleftiko..28
Kotopoulo me Hilopites...................................29
Kotopoulo me Rizi..29
Kouneli Stifado..30
Ntolmadakia me Kima.....................................30
Moussaka..31
Patatato...32
Yemista me Kima...32
Patsas..33
Piperia Gemisti..33
Psaronefri me Damaskina...............................34
Stifado...34
Soutzoukakia...35
Souvlaki...36
Tigania...36

RICE, PASTA, AND GRAIN DISHES

Hilopites...39
Kritharoto...39
Makarounes..40
Rizogalo..40
Manestra...41
Spanakorizo..42
Rizopita...43

SEAFOOD DISHES

Astakos...46
Atherina..46
Fournisto...47
Fried Marides...47
Fried Sardines..48
Gouna...48
Kakavia...49

Marida Skaras..50
Octopus Krasato...50
Kalamarakia...51
Octopus Stifado..51
Psari Sto Fourno me Ladolemono......................................52
Sardeles Kefalonia...53
Psari Plaki...53
Sardeles Pastes...54
Xtapodi Ksidato...54

SOUPS AND LEGUMES

Gigantes Plaki...56
Fasolada...57
Kolokithosoupa..57
Louvana..58
Fakes Soupa...58
Psarosoupa...59
Revithia..59

SWEETS AND DESSERTS

Amygdalota...62
Halvas me Simigdali...62
Baklava...63
Galaktoboureko...64
Karithopita..65
Karydia me Syko..66
Kourabiedes..66
Loukoumades..67
Moustalevria...68
Sykomaïda..68
Pasteli..69
Paximadia...69
Portokalopita..70
Sokolatenia Troufakia..70

VEGETABLE AND SALAD DISHES

Chorta Vrasta...73
Dolmadakia...73
Fasolakia...74
Fried Horta..74
Gemista..75
Horiatiki Salata...75
Kolokithia me Avgolemono...76
Kolokithokeftedes..76
Ladera..77
Lemon Roasted Potatoes..77
Marathokeftedes..78
Marathopita..78
Melitzanes imam..79
Patates Yachni..79
Pligouri Salad...80
Prasorizo..80
Roka Salata...81
Soufiko...81
Strapatsada...82
Briam..82

Printed in Great Britain
by Amazon